To dear Tom

I thought you might find this useful.

Happy Birthday

From Toffee

The author with her two dogs: Lulah (Dardale Telulah, CDex, UDex, WDex, TD, a German Shepherd bitch); and Angus (Working Trials Champion Spinbrook Legionaire, CDex, UDex, WDex, TDex, PDex, a Working Sheepdog).

GUARD DOG TRAINING

Rosie Jones

The Crowood Press

First published in 1988 by
The Crowood Press
Ramsbury, Marlborough
Wiltshire SN8 2HE

British Library Cataloguing in Publication Data

Jones, Rosie
Guard dog training.
1. Guard dogs. Training
I. Title
636.7'0886

ISBN 1 85223 087 8

Dedication

For Vulcan, Bella, Angus and Lulah, four canine companions whose co-operation and patience in training situations has taught me so much.

Acknowledgements

There are many people in the field of dog training who have helped me over the years, whose names are too numerous to mention, and to whom I owe a debt of gratitude. In particular I wish to thank John Harding for his advice and help; he, together with his son Paul and his daughter Jeanette, helped to set up many of the photographic situations, for which I am most grateful. My daughter Megan also co-operated in some of the photographs. I was also grateful to receive help and advice from Keith Lake.

The photographs throughout were taken by Geoff Davis.

Typeset by Acorn Bookwork, Salisbury, Wiltshire
Printed in Great Britain by Ebenezer Baylis & Son Ltd, Worcester

Contents

1 What is a Guard Dog?

For hundreds of years man has used dogs to protect his flocks from natural predators. He has used the dog's natural instincts, retaining and breeding from those animals which showed a good ability to guard the flocks, and rejecting those which did not perform so well. Over the years various breeds have evolved which have strong natural guarding instincts.

Modern society has become much more urbanised, and there are fewer opportunities for dogs to exercise the instincts for which they were originally bred. However, at the same time society has become less law-abiding, so a greater need has arisen for man to find some way of protecting himself, his family and his property. This is an area where a dog of the right breed and temperament can perform a useful service. When natural ability is combined with adequate training, a dog becomes a powerful weapon. It must be stressed that like all weapons, a dog can be lethal, unless it is under full control at all times. This control comes only with thorough and unremitting training.

I suppose the general picture of a guard dog which many people have is one of a snarling brute that will bite anything that approaches. If a dog has this kind of reputation it will undoubtedly keep all but the most foolhardy of intruders away, along with anyone who might have a legitimate reason to be there. This image does not do justice to the exceptional ability of a well-trained dog which is under full control at all times.

A trained dog can be just as fierce and aggressive as an untrained dog when the occasion demands, yet a safe family companion at the same time. A trained dog can be so much more versatile: he can be taken anywhere, at any time; he can adapt himself and his talents to whatever any particular situation demands; and he is certainly much less stressful to live with. If the dog is under full control, the owner is free to concentrate on what is happening around him, and to decide on the best way to tackle a particular situation. Perhaps he sees a potentially threatening incident developing. It may be that the situation could be resolved by talking to the would-be miscreant. It would be too late to try talking if the dog had already attacked.

The uses to which a trained guard dog can be put are many and varied, starting at the very simplest level, where a dog might be expected merely to give warning of an unusual presence. He might be alerted by sound, indicated by a pricking of the ears; or by scent, when he will turn his nose in the direction of the scent. With this warning, the owner can take appropriate action. Perhaps switching on a light is all that is necessary to scare away the stranger; perhaps appearing in the garden will stop children who were hoping to do a bit of scrumping.

Maybe the dog will be required to indicate the approach of a stranger more forcefully, by barking. This in itself will normally act as a strong deterrent. Certainly the sound of a dog barking is likely to scare off a casual opportunist. Sneak thieves do not like to have attention drawn to their presence and they tend to move on to a quieter location to carry out their nefarious activities. The deterrent effect of the mere presence of a dog has been recognised by at least one insurance company, which now offers up to a twenty-five per cent discount on the cost of a household-contents policy where the household includes a dog. It has been recognised that a barking dog cannot be turned off quite as easily as a burglar alarm.

To take matters a stage further, a situation may arise in which you suspect the presence of an intruder, either in a building or in the grounds. For various reasons it may not be possible or advisable for you to check out such a presence yourself. A dog, however, can be trained to search out such an intruder, wherever

Fig 1 These may be a couple of harmless drunks, but Bren's presence keeps them from approaching too close to his mistress.

and however he may have concealed himself, and to indicate to you the whereabouts of that person by barking. Then you will be in a position to deal with the situation as appropriate.

From merely sounding the alarm, so that his owner can take action, the dog also offers protection as a deterrent. By his very presence and threat of further action in taking up an aggressive stance, he is capable of keeping most wrong-doers at bay. Certainly a big dog, standing his ground, barking and growling, is a threat not to be lightly ignored.

As a last resort, if the deterrent effect fails, the dog may be required to use his natural weapon, his teeth, to detain a person who has committed, or who is about to commit, a serious offence. It must be stressed that to allow a dog to attack another person is a serious act of aggression, and such action must only be undertaken as a last resort. In such a case you could be considered to have used the dog as a weapon, and the law lays strict guide-lines on the use of weapons. You may use only reasonable force to protect yourself, your family or your property. What constitutes reasonable force is open to different interpretations according to circumstances.

It should be apparent that the various functions of a guard dog are not independent of one another. Any dog that barks is capable of giving a warning. A barking dog is usually to some extent a deterrent. However, many dogs greet their friends by barking, so if yours is a particularly friendly dog, who thinks of everyone as a friend, the deterrent effect is less. By the same token, the fact that he does bark at everyone may still give him some deterrent power. A person whose inclinations are unlawful will not wish to have attention drawn to himself by a barking dog, however friendly that dog may be.

The degree to which a barking dog acts as a deterrent depends partly on the aggressiveness of his bark and partly on his size. Certainly a large aggressive dog acts as a strong deterrent. Equally, a small aggressive nimble dog can have a similar effect. After all if the dog can reach only your backside or even your ankle, a quick nip in either place can be extremely painful. A dog does not necessarily have to appear capable of tearing you limb from limb to be avoided!

The line between being a threat and actually carrying out that threat is a very fine one, especially with those breeds which have strong natural guarding instincts. Such a dog must be trained to use those instincts for your benefit, and always under your control. He must not be allowed to decide for himself when and how to use those instincts. It is important to remember the relationship between the various guarding activities, and to consider the effect of each aspect on the others. Certainly the full attack should be used only as a last resort, after the warning and deterrent functions have failed.

A good guard dog, at whatever the level of guarding, is not born but needs to be trained. Many dogs possess some degree of guarding instinct and may do a reasonable job naturally for most of the time. However, should you find yourself in a critical situation, this is not the time to find out that you and your dog have suffered a breakdown in communications, and that your dog has decided to do his own thing leaving you on your own to deal with a situation where his presence would be useful to say the least!

Training a dog for guard duties is not easy, neither is it quick. Several months of patient, consistent training will be required to produce a fully trained dog. If you do the job properly the reward should be a reliable, safe dog, willing and able to defend you, your family, and your property to the limits of his ability. At the same time, you will have peace of mind knowing that your dog can be expected to behave impeccably in whatever situation you and he find yourselves. This will come about only if your dog is fully and carefully trained.

Even a dog working full-time as a guard dog will require time off for rest and relaxation. If he is well-trained, this presents no problem, he can do whatever fits in with your life-style. He can go for walks, jogging in the park, to do the shopping, or stay at home with the family. If he cannot be trusted to behave in these situations, your only option may be to shut him away from contact with the rest of the world. If he is excluded from the fun part of your life, you can hardly complain if he decides to opt out at times from the work part of your life. I am firmly convinced that the dog who shares your life fully is more likely to give his all to his work – and to do this he must be safe, reliable, and trained.

Training is not only about hard work on your part. It can, and should be, an enjoyable experience, building up a tremendous rapport between you and your dog, resulting in a great feeling of team-work. You and your dog are going to be working together, but that does not mean that you cannot enjoy being together at the same time.

WHY A GUARD DOG?

You must assess your own character and situation honestly to decide whether you simply want a guard dog, or whether you actually *need* a guard dog as well. There is a great deal of difference between wanting and needing in this context. A fierce dog can be very much a status symbol in some circles, boosting his owner's macho image. If this is the role in which you see a guard dog, then please think again. A guard dog should not be seen as a prop to bolster your image, and his training and care will require a serious commitment. You may well have property which needs protection, but there are other ways of acquiring that protection. You could install sophisticated electronic equipment, such as burglar alarms, or pressure mats which activate a tape of dogs barking. You could employ someone to train a dog for you and to patrol your premises. If it is personal protection which you require, you could hire a minder. Only if you are prepared to accept the responsibility of a full-time commitment should you consider owning a dog, let alone a guard dog.

Responsibility starts when you acquire your dog, and carries on for the rest of his life, which may be ten or fifteen years hence. You must be prepared to look after his well-being, keeping him healthy and fit. Apart from the cost of his food, you must budget for preventative inoculations and vaccinations, including annual boosters, to say nothing of any veterinary treatment which may be required if your dog is ill or injured. You must keep him fit by regular daily exercise. This does not mean a quick trip round the block if the weather is fine, but regular sustained exercise, whatever the weather, with the distance measured in miles rather than minutes. If you don't have the time or the energy for this kind of exercise, then you won't have the time or energy to train your dog, with consequences which may be unhappy for you, but which will certainly be disastrous for your dog.

As well as your responsibility towards your dog, you also have a responsibility to your family. The arrival of a dog will affect the lives of each member of your family. Although you will, it is to be hoped, teach your dog to respect his position in the family, your family must also respect the dog's needs. He is not a toy, and must not be teased, nor disturbed when at rest. There will be occasions when you cannot spend time with your family because the dog needs your attention. Holidays will also need careful consideration – if you normally spend them abroad, your dog will not be able to accompany you, and you will have to make special arrangements for him while you are away. If you have a reliable colleague who can look after your dog in your absence, well and good; otherwise you will need to find a suitable boarding kennel. Some kennels are unable, or unwilling, to board guard dogs – and those which do are not cheap. You may well have a noisy time ahead of you, at least for a few weeks, since whilst your dog is learning to bark at the right time, you will also have to accept him barking at the wrong time.

As a dog owner you also have responsibilities to your neighbours and to the general public. You have a duty not to let him roam, nor to cause annoyance or damage. As the owner of a guard dog, you have the further responsibility of training him thoroughly, and of regularly assessing your training schedule so that the dog does not become a danger to anyone. Once you have awakened his guarding instincts, you must ensure that they are used only under your control, and that the dog is never left to decide for himself when and if to attack.

The society in which we live has developed through the establishment of laws and rules of generally accepted behaviour, which govern our lives and actions, and which are constantly changing. Since dogs have become part of that society, they also are included in the mass of laws, regulations, control orders and bye-laws which have been passed to ensure that we can all live reasonably safely and peacefully with our neighbours. It is your duty to ensure that you are aware of, and abide by, the laws in your locality governing firstly the keeping of dogs in general, and secondly the keeping and use of guard dogs. You have a responsibility not only to yourself and your dog, but also to every other dog owner, to ensure that you do nothing to add fuel to the campaign waged by the anti-dog faction within our society, whose aim is to remove dogs entirely from our lives. Society will not only be poorer if they are allowed to succeed, but also much less safe.

A partly or badly trained dog of any description can be at best a nuisance, at worst a danger to society. A partly or badly trained guard dog is undoubtedly a danger, both to his handler and to the public in general. An irresponsible dog owner is an equal menace. Make up your mind before you start that you will put in all the effort necessary to ensure that your dog, through adequate training, becomes safe and reliable. A properly trained dog with a responsible owner should be your aim. Only time and effort will allow you to reach that goal.

2 What Sort of Dog?

The first thing that you must decide is the extent of guarding you require from your dog. If you want him to act only as a watch-dog, warning of the presence of strangers, then obviously almost any dog that is alert and barks would be adequate. However, if you are going to require the dog to act as a deterrent then he must have the stature and the physical presence to be able to do so – this precludes at a stroke any of the smaller breeds. But since you are going to spend considerable time and energy in training your dog, it will be in your own best interests to start with suitable material. This means choosing a breed that not only produces dogs of the right size but which are also capable of accepting the training that you will be giving them. This means looking at dogs in the group which the Kennel Club has classified as the working group. Although not all breeds within this group will be suitable, the one characteristic which has been bred into them over the centuries is that they are happy to work in the service of man, and to this end accept training readily.

GERMAN SHEPHERD DOG

Within the working group the breed which has proved itself eminently suitable in any kind of guarding duties is the German Shepherd Dog (sometimes incorrectly called the Alsatian). This breed has shown itself to be most successful in carrying out the varied duties required by the police and armed forces.

The traits which have been bred into this dog over the years which make him so suitable start with his physical appearance – quite simply he looks the part. Characteristically, the German Shepherd Dog looks alert, ever-vigilant and missing nothing. A typical specimen will stand from 22 to 26 inches at the shoulder, depending on sex, and weigh anything up to a hundred pounds. Certainly enough dog to cause second thoughts about arguing with him! The reputation of the breed as a vicious dog liable to attack anything without warning, whilst entirely unjustified, serves as a useful extra deterrent. The fact that a German Shepherd Dog can be gentle enough to act as companion and guardian for a small child is not generally accepted by most burglars – thankfully, they usually accept the reputation and go elsewhere.

According to the Breed Standard, the German Shepherd Dog

'has a distinct personality marked by direct and fearless, but not hostile, expression, self-confidence and a certain aloofness that does not lend itself to immediate and indiscriminate friendships . . . Three of the most outstanding traits are incorruptibility, discernment and ability to reason'.

This breed is typically a 'one-man dog' and is happiest when he gives his

Fig 2 Bren shows the alertness of a typical German Shepherd Dog.

allegiance to one person, whom he will serve to the best of his ability, giving his life if necessary to protect that person. In order to gain his allegiance, you must earn it – it cannot be bought. He will give it to the person who trains him (if it is done correctly) and not necessarily to the person who feeds him.

ROTTWEILER

The Rottweiler is another breed which can be most suitable for training as a guard dog. He stands about the same height as a German Shepherd Dog, but is of a more compact appearance. In looks he is powerful and stalwart, with a demeanour which is dignified and shows boldness and courage. He possesses the characteristic traits of this group of dogs, being intelligent, easily trained, naturally obedient, and extremely devoted to those who merit his affection. Although he may appear tranquil and good-natured when in the company of those he loves and respects, just let anyone threaten him or his pack, and take the consequences! His somewhat lumbering gait disguises an ability to cover the ground

Fig 3 At eleven months of age, Bear already shows the compact power of the Rottweiler.

extremely swiftly if he has a purpose for doing so. The Rottweiler tends to be a dog who gives his all when necessary, but who otherwise prefers to take life at a stately pace.

DOBERMANN

Another breed which has been used extensively in the past for guard duties is the Dobermann, although it seems to be less fashionable at present. One of the reasons given for its decline in popularity is that whilst a good Dobermann is very good, it is easier to find a poor specimen than a good one. This breed will grow to around the same height as the two previous breeds, but is more lightly built than the Rottweiler. Again the Dobermann is compactly built, muscular and powerful, with a proud carriage, showing alertness, a certain elegance and undoubted determination. He is loyal and obedient when carefully handled and trained.

These three breeds have over the years become the most popular for training as guard dogs. They have proved themselves eminently suitable, by virtue of

Fig 4 Gary shows the muscular elegance of the Dobermann.

their inherent characteristics of loyalty, determination, fearlessness and obedience. However, there are other breeds within the working group which have been successfully trained as guard dogs. These include the Boxer, the Giant Schnauzer, the Bouvier des Flandres and the Belgian Shepherd Dog, particularly the Tervueren. It is important that you like both the breed you choose and the particular individual. You will not make a successful partnership if you choose a suitable breed which actually has an appearance that you dislike.

There is one more breed that perhaps ought to be mentioned, and that is the Border Collie, also known as the Working Sheep Dog or Working Collie. This breed possesses all the useful characteristics of the working group, but unfortunately it lacks the imposing stature of the previously mentioned breeds. However, if a watch-dog is required, capable of indicating the presence of strangers, more than actually driving them off, then the collie could certainly be considered. He is very easily trained, quick to learn, in fact almost too quick sometimes. He can be excitable and may require calm handling. He is capable of working on his own initiative and has great stamina.

Fig 5 Angus, a well-built Collie–this is a breed that is quick to learn and easy to train, but which lacks the physical stature of some of the other working breeds.

PUPPY OR ADULT?

Having made your choice of breed, the next question is whether to look for a puppy or an adult dog of that breed.

The Adult Dog

The main advantage of the adult dog is the fact that he will be mature enough to undertake a fairly intensive training course as soon as he has settled in with you. This means that if your training is successful, he will be fully operational as a guard dog much sooner than would a puppy. However, set against that is the fact that you will not know what experiences he has undergone whilst growing up. After all, if an adult dog becomes available for you to take on, there will normally be a good reason for him requiring a new home. It may be that his previous owner is simply unable to keep him, whether through ill-health or changed circumstances, in which case you may acquire a good dog. On the other hand the previous owner may be getting rid of the dog because he has become out-of-hand. Again it may be that all he needs is sound, careful training.

Even so, he may have been allowed to develop all kinds of bad habits, in which case you will have to spend a lot of time eradicating these and overcoming bad experiences before you can start to progress with the training needed to turn the dog into a useful guard dog. Beware of the kind of advertisement which says something like 'Free to good home, make good guard dog'. Good guard dogs do not come 'free', and if you eventually train a dog successfully to become a good guard dog, you will know that the time and effort needed puts his value into the extremely expensive bracket, if not even beyond price.

The Puppy

If you start with a puppy, say seven to ten weeks old, which is the usual age for a puppy to leave his dam, you will have to wait something like a year before you can expect him to work for you. On the other hand you will be starting with a virtually blank canvas, and so can make sure that the puppy learns only those things that will be useful, and is not allowed to develop any undesirable habits as he grows up. You will be able to develop that special bond between you which makes a successful partnership. If the puppy grows up with you, he will get to know you so well that it will appear that he can almost read your mind, and you his.

An adult dog should be able to concentrate for longer periods of time than would a puppy. However, he may not have learned to concentrate, or even how to learn, so you may have to spend time teaching him how to accept training. If you bring up a puppy in the recommended way and carry out the pre-training exercises, he will already be conditioned to the right attitude when he becomes old enough for more intensive training.

DOG OR BITCH?

The next decision you will have to make is whether to choose a dog or a bitch. On the whole a dog will be about two inches taller than a bitch of the same breed, and weigh perhaps ten or twenty pounds more. This obviously gives the dog greater presence as a deterrent. Bitches tend to be more affectionate, whilst dogs often have a more independent streak.

The one major difference between the sexes is that a bitch, once mature, will come into season (on heat) approximately twice a year. Each season lasts about three to four weeks. During this time she will not be able to work as she will need to be closely confined so that she is not mated by a visiting canine Romeo. The season can be either stopped or prevented, by the use of drugs or surgery. Your veterinary surgeon will advise you on the best method for your particular needs. Although a dog does not have seasons, he may be affected by a neighbouring bitch in season, in which case his work may suffer. Castration sometimes cures an excessive interest in the opposite sex if carried out at the right time – again your veterinary surgeon is the person to consult.

In the sphere of guard dog duties, dogs far outnumber bitches. That is not to say that there are not some very capable bitches, and indeed a good bitch is to be much preferred to a mediocre dog. As with choosing the breed, it is important to choose the sex with which you will be happiest. Some people prefer to work a dog, others are happiest with a bitch. What matters in the last analysis is that you feel right together as a team.

TEMPERAMENT

The temperament of the animal you finally choose is of vital importance. Choosing an adult could show you what you are getting, but without knowing the background of the dog you will be unable to tell if, for instance, an unruly dog behaves that way because of poor temperament or because he has not had the opportunity to learn how to behave in a civilised manner. Remember that it is not in the nature of some breeds, particularly the German Shepherd, to be overly friendly with strangers. However, he should be confident enough to meet any overtures you make without making any himself. Any signs of cringing, tucking of the tail or an anxious expression, whilst possible evidence of ill-treatment, are also signs of poor temperament, as is an aggressive attitude.

If you look for a puppy, you should expect the whole litter to be friendly and outgoing. If they all rush out to vie for your attention, that is an excellent sign. Try to have a look at both the parents of the puppies. You must insist on seeing at least the dam, as her attitude to life in general will affect the way in which the puppies view the world. If she is confident and secure then there is a good chance that the puppies will grow up in the same way. If she is afraid of her own shadow, then the pups will already have learned that the world can be a frightening place. A dog who is continually looking over his shoulder expecting trouble will not be able to concentrate fully on the job for which you are going to train him.

If you go to a reputable breeder and explain exactly what you are looking for, you should find him helpful in your choice. It may be in fact that his particular strain, whilst of sound temperament, will turn out to be too 'soft' for your purposes, and a reputable breeder will tell you so. If you are offered an older dog, try to find out exactly why he is being offered. There are many excellent reasons why an adult dog is looking for a new home, but there are as many bad reasons. What you must try to ensure is that you end up with a dog which, when adult, will be bold but biddable, confident without being over-aggressive, and definitely a dog that you like and will enjoy working with.

HEALTH

It goes without saying that whatever age or breed of dog you choose, it must be physically fit, and free from any signs of ill-health. Its construction needs to be sound, and whilst minor defects are not important, it must conform fairly closely to the relevant breed standard. For instance, any variation from the normal height: weight ratio could lead to spinal problems. A pedigree by itself, no matter how many champions it contains, will not guarantee a sound dog, but it can improve your chances. For example, where a particular line is known to be H.D. (hip dysplasia) free for several generations, there is a greater chance of avoiding this defect than from a line where there have been cases in recent generations. Certain lines are known to carry an increased predisposition towards fits and obviously these should be avoided.

Try to gain as much information about the breeding of your potential dog before making your final choice, and get your veterinary surgeon to check the animal over before committing yourself. You are going to put a lot of time and effort into training your dog, and it would be a waste to train a dog which will have a short working life because of inherited defects or poor conformation. However carefully you check, it is not possible to guarantee that a dog will have a long and trouble-free working life. If you start with a sound healthy animal, and look after it well, you will at least reduce the odds against a shortened working life as much as possible.

3 Equipment

From the start you will need a certain amount of equipment in order to look after your dog properly, be he a puppy or an adult. First of all you will need feeding utensils. From a hygiene point of view it is better if the dog has his own set, rather than using general household dishes. He will also need a water bowl. If he will later be working away from home he will need separate water dishes in the vehicle you use for transport and at his place of work. You will also need a set of grooming tools – a soft brush for a puppy, graduating to a normal brush or comb as he matures. If as a working dog he is going to be outside in all weathers, you will need a supply of towels with which to dry him down. Old ones will do, it is not advisable to raid the household linen cupboard!

The next decision to make is where the dog will sleep and spend his off-duty hours. If he is eventually to work a full shift, he must have a quiet place of his own to rest in when he comes home. If you cannot find such a place in the house, or if you have a noisy family, perhaps an outside run and kennel might be the answer. Make sure the kennel has draught-free and weather-proof sleeping quarters. If your dog is to sleep in the house make sure he has a spot which is his own. He does not need an elaborate bed; in fact a blanket in a quiet corner is probably better so that he can stretch out as he wishes. A specially bought dog bed would have to be very large to allow this.

Wherever he sleeps, your dog must be allowed to spend at least part of his off-duty time with you. Certainly a puppy should not be left out in a kennel for long periods. He needs to be with you and your family so that he can become accustomed to normal household noises and activities. He will get used to sudden noises and movements, and to meeting the various people who visit the house. This is an important aspect of socialisation for a dog, which can take place without any conscious effort on your part. A dog left for long periods on his own can soon become bored, and then make a nuisance of himself by barking, howling or chewing. In any case a dog is more use to you if he is allowed in the home – how can he protect you from burglars if he is shut outside in a kennel or run?

EQUIPMENT FOR TRAINING

Collar

Your pup will almost immediately need a soft house collar. This is simply a lightweight collar that he wears all the time, and is not for attaching a lead. It is simply so that in your pre-training exercises you can restrain him when necessary. Make sure that it fits snugly, without a dangling end to irritate him, and check regularly that it is not too tight. It will not last long; pups grow so fast that he will require two or three before he

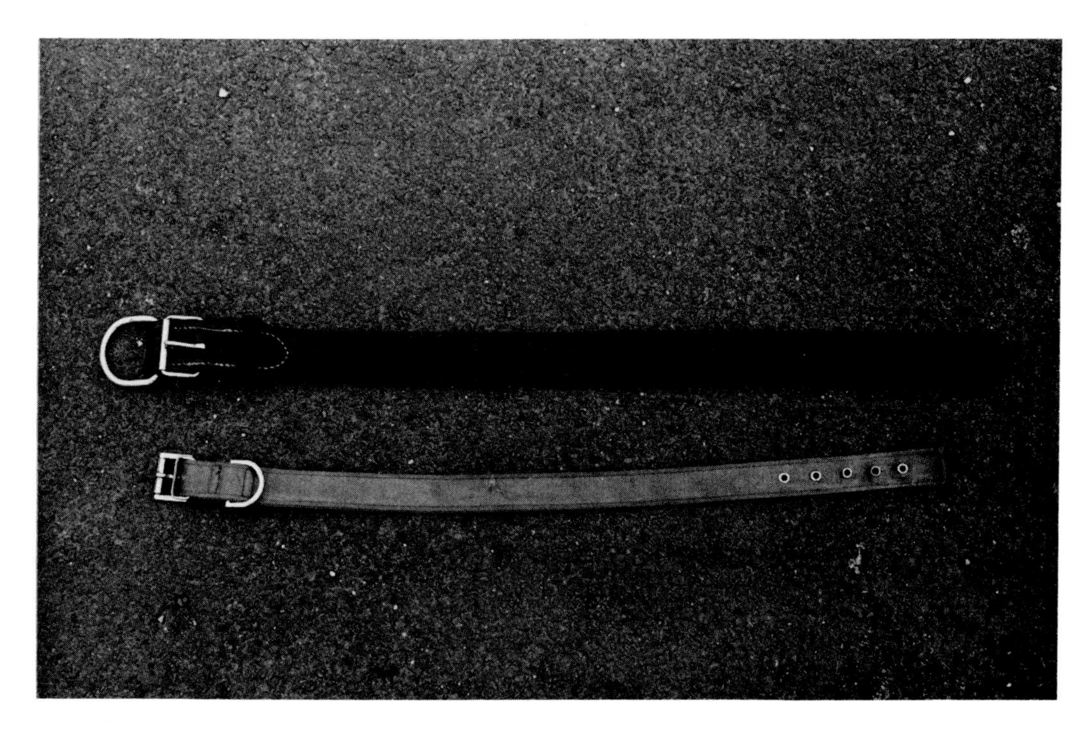

Fig 6 A leather collar (above) and a webbing collar (below), both with adjustable buckles and sturdy rings.

Fig 7 Check-chains with different sized links.

Fig 8 Passing the check-chain through one of its end rings, to form the loop which goes over the dog's head.

grows into his proper training collar.

When he is old enough for serious training he will need a more substantial collar. This can be either leather or webbing and again should fit comfortably, but not so slack that he can pull his head through. It must be well stitched and have a robust buckle and ring to which you can attach the lead. It will need to be adjustable, as he will still have some growing to do. Check the fit regularly. If at a later stage you consider a check-chain to be necessary, again choose a robust one. Don't use too fine a link – it will act more as a cheese-wire than a check.

In order that it can act as a check, and not as a choker, it must be put on correctly. Make sure that when the dog is on your left (the usual working side), the end that is attached to the lead goes across the top of his neck. In this way it

Fig 9 Lulah demonstrates the correct way to wear a check-chain.

Fig 10 A rope lead, showing a strong trigger hook.

Fig 11 A leather training lead, with intermediate rings for adjusting the length.

Fig 12 A long line, with trigger hook attached.

will slacken off after being used to check the dog. Otherwise it will remain tight, and therefore ineffectual, once it has been used as a check. A check-chain must only be used when it has a lead attached and when you are holding the lead. It must not be used for tethering a dog, because of the very real possibility of the dog damaging his neck or even strangling himself.

Lead

The lead can be of leather, rope or webbing. Again it must be well made, with a robust trigger clip securely attached. Webbing leads can have sharp edges, and so be rather hard on your hands. Don't be tempted to buy a chain lead. It may seem very substantial, but it will be very hard on your hands, and is too inflexible to be a sensitive means of communication between you and your dog.

Leads come in various lengths and you will need one at least three feet in length. The kind called a training lead is about six foot long, with an extra trigger hook at the holding end and a ring half way along so that it can be used either at full length or clipped back to half length. A training lead may come in useful in later stages of training.

A long line may be required if your dog is slow to learn to recall to you. This is a length of rope with a trigger hook at one end and a loop for you to hold at the

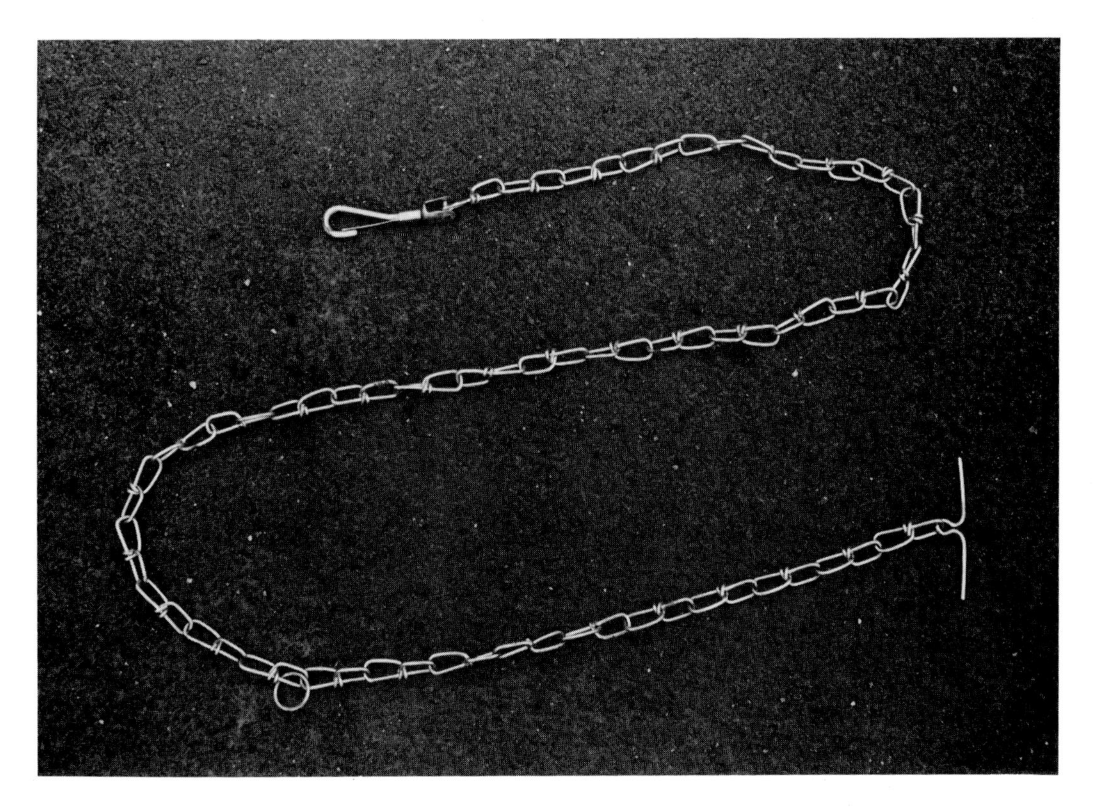

Fig 13 A chain suitable for securing a heavy dog.

other. If you need to tie your dog up during training, a chain is useful, being stronger than a lead. Again it should have a strong trigger hook at one end and some means of fastening it round a post or bar at the other.

TRAVELLING

If your dog will have to travel much to carry out his duties, do give some thought to his comfort during transportation. It is a good idea to have a cage fitted into your vehicle, for the dog to travel in. As long as it is roomy enough for him to turn round in, he will in fact travel more comfortably than if he were loose in the back of your vehicle. For safety reasons a dog should never travel in the front of a vehicle.

It is possible to buy cages to fit most makes of car or van, and also a dividing partition, so that two dogs may be transported together safely. If your dog has to spend any length of time in your vehicle whilst it is parked, with one of these cages fitted you will be able to leave the back door open safely, as well as windows, thus ensuring a through draught of air to keep the temperature down. Even so, only leave your dog in the vehicle when you can park in the shade. It takes very little time for a vehicle to become dangerously over-heated, even without the sun being out. If your vehicle

Fig 14 A travelling cage, with divider for carrying two adult dogs.

is a van, it is a good idea to have a ventilator fitted to help keep the interior cool, as a van is usually less well insulated than a car.

SPECIALISED EQUIPMENT

If you are going to train your dog for full guard duties, that is to attack, then you will need a range of equipment to protect the person who is to act as your 'criminal'. To start your training you will need a *flag*, which is a piece of sacking with one end rolled up and taped to form a handle. You can if you wish make this more elaborate by stuffing the sacking so that it becomes a sausage-shape, or you can in fact buy a ready-made *bar*, which has a hand-grip and wrist-strap.

Sleeves

By convention dogs are taught to bite the right forearm of their victim, at least in training as otherwise you would soon run out of helpers! To protect this part of the arm, you will need a selection of padded *sleeves*. These can be made of various materials and give differing degrees of protection according to how thickly they are padded. To start with you will need a very soft sleeve, made of hessian or jute. Later you will progress to one or more leather sleeves as your dog's bite develops. These can be either elbow-length or longer to protect the

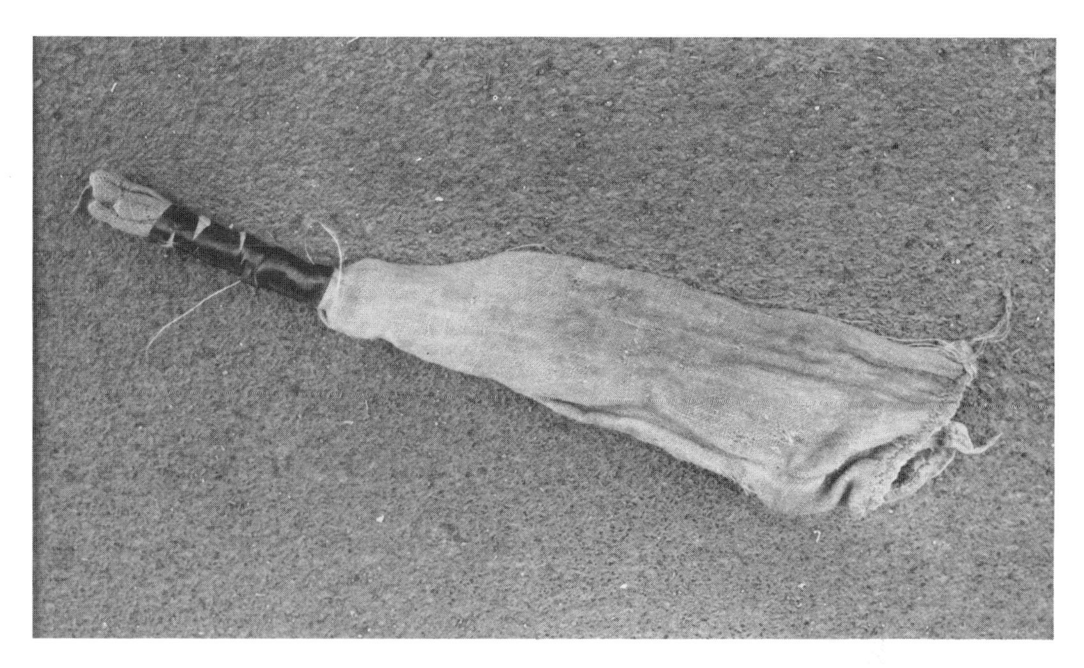

Fig 15 The flag, with taped handle.

Fig 16 The bar, with handle and wrist-strap.

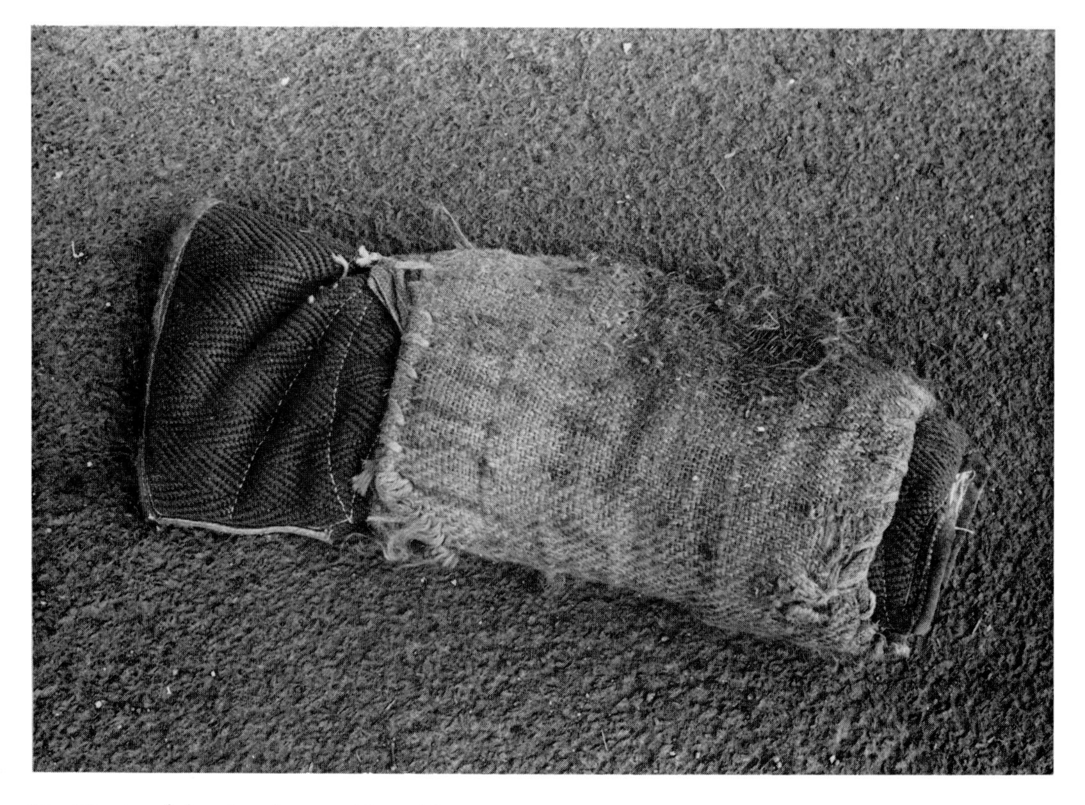

Fig 17 A soft hessian sleeve, with sacking cover.

upper arm, with a hinge at the elbow for ease of movement. Sleeves can also be obtained with a flap to cover the hand.

As sleeves are expensive pieces of equipment they should be looked after so that they give years of service. If a dog is allowed to bite directly on to the leather it will not last long. In any case the leather would soon become wet from the dog's saliva, and therefore slippery and difficult for the dog to grip. To solve this problem, you will need a supply of sacking with which to cover the biting area of the sleeve, and a sail-maker's needle and thread with which to attach it. This sacking cover will not last long, but is easily replaced, and much cheaper than a new sleeve.

THE TRAINER

Perhaps the most important item of equipment of all is you, the trainer. Unless you are the right kind of person, you will not make a success of training your dog. You must have absolute self-control, so that no matter what happens you *never* lose your temper with your dog. If things go wrong it will be because you have failed in some way to organise the training session correctly. Self-criticism is a necessary attribute of a successful trainer.

Patience is a virtue which you will need in abundance, as for every two or three steps that you take forwards, you

Fig 18 A leather sleeve, hinged at the elbow, again with sacking cover.

Fig 19 A leather sleeve with hand cover.

will almost certainly take at least one backwards. In some weeks you may even feel that the only way you are progressing is totally backwards! You need to be dedicated and self-disciplined if you are to undertake the training of your dog. You face months of hard work, and must be prepared to carry out your daily training sessions no matter what the weather or what is on the television. Even when your dog is mature and has started to work for you, his training does not finish – he will need regular refresher sessions, right to the end of his working life.

As a good trainer you must be consistent, always giving commands in the same manner. At the same time you need to be adaptable, so that you can react quickly to changing responses from your dog. And in addition to these mental attributes, you must also be physically fit. The kind of training you will be undertaking will make considerable demands on your stamina. Finally, you need to be able to inspire some friends to help you. The later stages of training require the co-operation of several helpers, without whom you will not be able to complete the training of your guard dog. You must be able to communicate your instructions to them clearly if your dog is not to become confused.

If self-examination reveals any defects in your character, then please do not proceed any further, at least until you have taken yourself in hand. You will otherwise cause yourself a great deal of trouble, and what is more a great deal of misery for your dog. Remember, you have a choice – he does not.

4 Elementary Training

The training techniques in this chapter assume that you have chosen a puppy. If you are in fact training an older dog, then the training programme will be the same, but you may well proceed at a different rate. Sometimes you will be able to progress faster, at others you may have to take time out to cure faults which your dog has previously developed. At all times you must adjust your progress to the needs of your dog, and his ability to continue with the training. If you seem to make no progress one day, then forget training for that day. Dogs can have off-days as well as humans! For clarity we shall also assume that you have chosen a male – the training applies equally to bitches.

The most important lesson to teach your pup in the early stages is that life with you is enjoyable, and you are the centre of his universe. For this to be true, you must *be* the centre of his universe. This means giving him your full attention whilst he is with you, and making the effort to spend most of his waking hours together. This will not be such a great deal of time in the early days, as a young puppy spends much of his time asleep, but it is important that you arrange your life so that you can spend as much time as possible with him.

Hopefully the puppy you have chosen will be very curious and gregarious; he will want to be with you, to join in with whatever you happen to be doing. Do make every opportunity for your pup to be with you, but at the same time, make time to play with him, and to join in his games. The games you play with him can be a very useful pre-training conditioning.

INTRODUCING THE TUGGER

One game that is enjoyable for the puppy, and most useful as an aid to later training, is a tug of war with a piece of rag. Make sure that it is strong enough to stand the strain of the puppy pulling against you, and long enough for you to get a comfortable hold of the end opposite to him. The leg of an old pair of jeans is very suitable for this game. You can introduce the game after a few days, when your pup has settled into his new home. Make sure that it is a game you play together – don't allow the pup to take this *tugger* off to play by himself. You must obviously adjust your pull to his strength, allowing him to pull you and win most of the time to begin with, only increasing your pull as his confidence grows. You can gradually make him work harder to pull you.

Start off in a confined space, so that if he decides to run off to chew the tugger the first time he wins it, you can make a game of catching him and repeating the tug. He will soon learn that it is more fun to return for another game, as long as you keep it light-hearted and don't make an issue if he does carry off his trophy at first.

It is important at this stage that *you* decide when the game shall end. Keep it short to start with, and always leave the pup wanting more. Several short games during the day are much more useful than the same amount of time spent in one prolonged game. The idea you want to get over is that this is a special treat you are allowing your puppy, not something he must do.

When you decide to end the game, you must take possession of the tugger. To do this, make sure you have a firm grasp of it. Stop all movement at your end, and say firmly 'leave'. Remember that to speak firmly does not mean to shout or browbeat. Probably the shock of your firm command together with the tugger going dead will be enough to cause the pup to release his grasp. Quickly remove the tugger and tell the pup what a clever dog he is. Be very generous in your praise – he must be quite sure that he has done the right thing for the time being, as you will want him to come back for another game very shortly. If he does not release the tugger immediately, carefully open his mouth by pressing his lower lips gently against his teeth, and remove the tugger as before. Again praise lavishly.

It is important that you get an instant response to the command 'leave'. Do not repeat it, and always make sure you are in a position to enforce it if necessary. This is one of the most important lessons that your pup has to learn – not merely the meaning of the command, but that when you give a command you will give it once only, expecting (and enforcing) instant obedience. You must also learn this lesson. The success or otherwise of your training depends on your ability to abide by this golden rule – give a command once only and insist that it is obeyed.

Think of the difference if you repeat the command say half a dozen times before insisting on obedience. This can only lead to confusion in your dog's mind. On five occasions the command means nothing and may safely be ignored, but on the sixth occasion the same command is to be obeyed. Unless your dog is exceptionally clever at counting, he will never know whether the command is one of the five times to be ignored or the sixth one to be obeyed. A confused dog is an unreliable dog, so from the start, teach yourself to give a command once only and make sure that you are in a position to ensure it is obeyed.

Don't 'test' your dog to see if he will obey. Assume he will not and always be prepared to take the necessary action. If the dog always obeys your commands instantly, because you give him no choice, instant obedience will become automatic, and there is no reason why he should ever disobey, unless in very exceptional circumstances. When your dog starts to anticipate your actions, and reacts to the command a fraction quicker than you do, then you can be pleasantly surprised, and increase your praise accordingly. Since your dog will always obey a command (with or without your help), he will always merit praise, and must always receive it. Remember you are praising the result (over which you have control) not the intention.

Although this is a game in the early stages, it will have far-reaching consequences for your later training. First of all

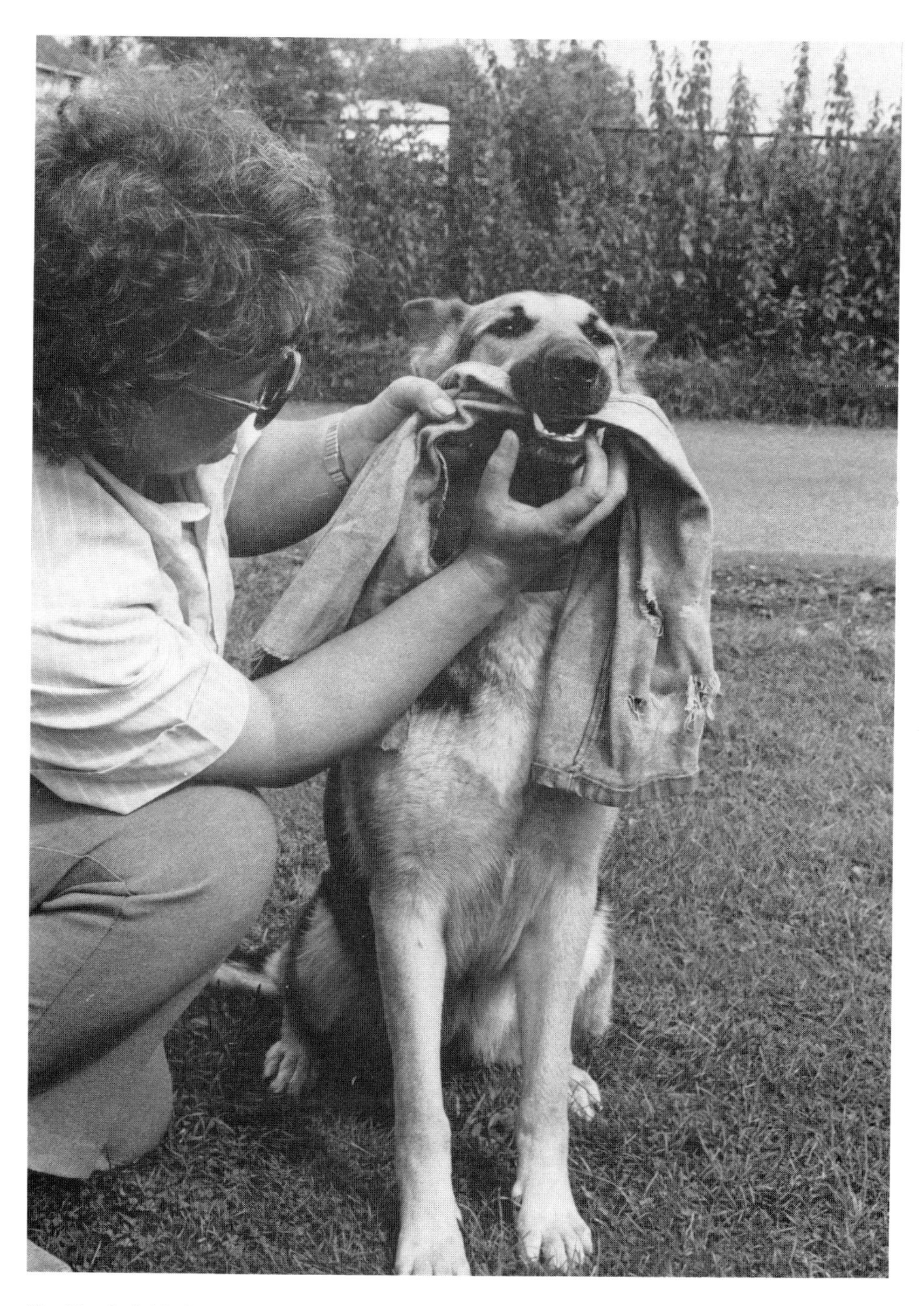

Fig 20 Lulah's lips are gently pressed against her teeth to encourage her to release the tugger.

it is fun, so starts building up your relationship with your dog, and can be used as a reward later when he carries out more advanced exercises. Secondly, it is the start of obedience, teaching the dog that you are in charge, and when you give a command, it must be obeyed. It also gets you into the habit of self-discipline. When you give a command, you will give it once only, and it must always be obeyed. Remember that if you are not in a position to enforce a command, do not give it. Wait until a more suitable occasion.

You must be extremely careful with this game whenever your puppy is teething. If he should experience pain at this time he may be reluctant to play again. Be guided by your pup's attitude – if he wants to continue to play, then do so very gently. If he would rather not, then postpone the games until he has completed the teething process.

TEACHING THE DOWN

Another exercise to teach your pup very early is to lie down and to remain in that position until you say he may move. This exercise is usually known as the *down stay*. The exercise is useful in its own right – there will be many occasions when you will want your dog to remain in the down position whilst you attend to whatever you have to do. It is also a submissive position, so teaching and enforcing it also reinforces the idea that you are the dominant half of the partnership. Again this exercise can be started once your puppy has had a few days to settle in with you. It is relatively easy to push a small pup into the down position, using the command 'down', and to hold him there with light finger pressure for a second or two. Praise him, even if he is struggling to get up, then release him. Make it clear to him that he is released from the command. I usually say 'O.K., finish' when I release my dog from an exercise. You need a word or phrase to tell your dog that the exercise is over and he may relax. Choose something now and use it every time you release your dog from an exercise.

Timing

Repeat this down exercise several times during the next few days, at first insisting on obedience for only a second or two. Gradually increase the length of time from a few seconds to a few minutes, then eventually up to thirty minutes. You will need to get down to the pup's level for this training, which means either sitting or kneeling beside him, so it is best started in the house. As you increase the time element, you can settle in front of the television, or with a book.

In the early stages you should keep a hand on his shoulder, to ensure that he stays down. You will be able to feel any resistance on his part, and prevent it from developing into disobedience. Remember, in no circumstances must he be allowed to get up until you decide the exercise is complete and give him his release signal. Try to ensure that you will not be interrupted. If for instance the telephone rings and you must answer it, you *must* release the pup first, even if the exercise has not lasted as long as you intended. Don't try him out, thinking you can keep an eye on him whilst you answer the call. Terminate the exercise, deal with the interruption and then start again later. If your puppy should ever be allowed to decide for himself when to get up, you will have negated a whole lot of training, and will have to start all over again.

If as you increase the time in the down, your pup actually goes to sleep during the exercise, don't worry. When the time is up, wake him gently and then release him. It is important not to leave him whilst he is asleep, because if you allow him to get up when he wakes up, he will have decided for himself when to terminate the down stay. It may not have been a conscious decision, but it will nevertheless be a decision made by him, and that puts him in charge.

We have assumed so far that your puppy is co-operative and is easily pushed into the down position. If he is not sufficiently co-operative, there are other ways of insisting that he goes down. First of all you can use his tugger. Get down beside him, with him on your left-hand side. Hold his collar with your left hand and with your right hand place his tugger on the ground a few inches in front of him. As his head goes down to investigate, your left hand prevents forward movement and he should collapse quite easily. Don't forget to give your command as he assumes the position.

Teaching an Older Dog

Both of these methods rely on the fact that a young puppy is not particularly well co-ordinated, and so cannot resist the slight pressure you apply. If he is somewhat older, and more in control of himself, the following method may be

Fig 21 The tugger used to encourage puppy Belle to go down.

Fig 22 Angus demonstrates the stages from the sit to the down: his handler's right hand grasps his front leg . . .

Fig 23 . . . the left hand pushes his shoulders to unbalance him . . .

useful. Again start by getting down to his level, and have him sitting on your left. This time hold his collar with your left hand, and with your right hand grasp his left foreleg. Gently push this leg forwards, at the same time using your left hand (still on his collar) to push his shoulders away from you. Make sure he is not able to get up and move forwards. The combination of his front leg moving forwards and his shoulders moving sideways should put him sufficiently off-balance to enable you to ease him into the down position. If he manages to lift his backside from the floor, carry on as before. Once his head and shoulders are on the ground and held there, he will find it very uncomfortable to keep his backend up. Keep his front end firmly down with your right hand, and if necessary take your left hand back to push his backside down.

Fig 24 . . . the down completed.

Remember to give your command as you start the movement. Do not repeat it, however long it takes to complete the action, and do not give in until you have succeeded. No matter how much the dog struggles, he must realise once and for all that when you give a command, it will be obeyed. Don't lose your temper, but quietly continue to ease him into position. However long it takes, you must hold his head and shoulders down until he gives in. Once he is completely down, hold him there for only a second or two, praise him, and release him as before. If you have had a struggle to get him down, there is a strong temptation to keep him down for a length of time. Do resist this temptation – you will make faster and more reliable progress in the long run if you release him quickly. Once he realises that all you require of him at the moment is that he assumes the down position on command, he will have less reason to resist you the next time.

Give him a few minutes play, then start the sequence all over again. Don't try to increase the time you ask him to stay down until he is going down quickly on command without resistance. Although he may still require help to go down, he should very soon accept this help without struggling. Once he goes down on command (with or without help from you) you can rapidly increase the time you keep him in the down position, until you have built the time up to thirty minutes as before. Try to vary the length of time that you keep him down, including one or two shorter stays every so often. In this way you keep his interest as you do not become predictable. Dogs seem to have an in-built clock and if you always do a ten minute down, for example, you could soon find that your dog will do ten minutes happily, but start to break his stay if you leave him for ten minutes and thirty seconds!

As your dog becomes more reliable, you will gradually be able to reduce the amount of pressure you apply to keep him down. You must then become even more alert as you will not be able to 'feel' him thinking about getting up. Watch him carefully, and the instant he starts to think about moving, increase the pressure of your hand just sufficiently to keep him in place. Remember it is vital to take action *before* he moves. Once he has moved it is too late, so don't get too involved in that television programme!

Changing Location

Once your puppy is going down and staying down reliably in the house, you can start to introduce new locations – another room, the garden, the local park. Start again from the beginning with each new location. If you have done your early training thoroughly, you will be able to progress very rapidly. Of course how you progress in different locations will depend to a certain extent on the time of year. Don't ask a young pup to stay down for more than a few seconds if the ground is very wet, very hot or very cold. To insist on a longer stay in such conditions would distress the puppy, and therefore be counter-productive. Whilst a mature trained dog might reasonably be expected to endure a certain amount of discomfort if it is necessary for him to be left lying on cold, wet or hot ground for a short while, there is no need to make training a miserable experience for your puppy.

Fig 25 Belle's handler takes a coffee into the garden to help pass the time while Belle practises her down.

Increasing Distance

Gradually increase the distance between you when your pup will stay down for thirty minutes. The first time you try to move, it is almost certain that your pup will try to move with you. Be prepared, and make sure he does not succeed. Perhaps the best thing to do the first time is simply to change your position from sitting to kneeling beside him. In this way you can keep your hand on him ready to prevent any movement. Then you might sit in a chair, with your dog lying beside you.

As you increase the distance between you, you must be ever more alert. The secret is to read your dog's mind, and to take action at the moment he thinks about moving, before he actually moves. If you watch your dog carefully, you will get to know the signs. So long as he is never allowed to get beyond the 'thinking' stage, he will accept that you really can read his mind, and so you should have less trouble later.

Although the length of time you require your dog to stay down will be built up quite rapidly, distancing yourself from him must happen much more slowly. Once you can safely stand up beside your dog, you can take a step away from him for a second, then return to complete the time of the stay. Remember that your dog will become reliable in this exercise only if he is never

Fig 26 At twelve weeks old, Belle is already becoming reliable in the down stay.

Fig 27 The tugger used to help Belle to sit.

allowed to move from the down until you say so. The importance of this exercise is not only as an exercise in itself, but if well taught, it establishes the future relationship between you and your dog. It confirms the pack order, with you in control, and the dog as a willing and obedient pack member.

THE SIT

You will need to put your dog into the sit position before commencing many of the following exercises, so teach it as soon as possible. Choose your word of command carefully – so often one hears a dog being told to 'sit down'. How is he to know whether you mean him to sit or to go down? As with the down, make sure he sits when you give the command and remains in that position until you release him.

Again you can use the pup's lack of co-ordination in the early stages. Holding his tugger above his head should cause him to sit, as you give the command. If more help is needed, get down to his level. Hold his collar in your right hand and use your left forearm to apply slight pressure to his stifle joints (knees). If you have ever been hit by a football (or a dog!) at the back of your knees, you will know the sudden feeling of collapse.

Fig 28 Lulah demonstrates the stages in moving from the stand to the sit: her handler's hand ready to apply pressure to her stifle-joints . . .

Fig 29 . . . nearly there . . .

Fig 30 . . . the sit completed.

Fig 31 Lulah (on the left) demonstrates the down stay with Angus in the sit stay, in spite of the distraction of a football.

Fig 32 Once released from the stay, Lulah and Angus enjoy a game with the football.

This is the effect you will be trying to achieve, but gently of course. Once in the sit, hold him there, praise him and release him after a few seconds, using your release signal. As with the down, gradually increase the time you require him to sit, up to perhaps three or four minutes. There is no need to lengthen it to thirty minutes as you are not trying to establish pack leadership. Again as with the down, when he is steady by your side, gradually stand up, and then move away. Don't let him move, and don't let him slide into the down, even at the end of the exercise. Remember the golden rule, and insist on instant obedience every time you give a command.

THE STAND

There may be occasions when you will wish your dog to stay where he is, without necessarily adopting either the sit or the down position. Therefore it is useful to teach the stand stay. For this exercise the dog is placed in the stand position, and is required to stay still until released. If the pup is standing, hold his collar with your right hand, and place your left hand, palm down, under his belly as you give the command 'stand'. Praise, and release him as before. Don't stand over him, but get down to his level, so that he does not feel threatened.

If you start this exercise with your pup

Fig 33 Lulah demonstrates the stages from the sit to the stand: her handler's hand underneath her belly . . .

Fig 34 . . . to apply pressure to her upper thigh . . .

Fig 35 . . . and Lulah completes the stand.

Fig 36 Belle is held whilst her handler uses the tugger to encourage the recall.

in the sit position, get down as before, hold his collar with your right hand, and place your left hand palm down under his belly. Gently slide your left hand back so that you can apply slight pressure to his upper thigh and stifle joints, in order to bring the dog into the stand. There is no point in extending the time for more than a minute or so, because this position will be used only as a temporary measure in order to halt your dog so that you can give an alternative instruction. In any case it is not a stable position, nor a comfortable one, so it would be unkind to insist on a lengthy stand stay. Having said that, the stay command must always be implicitly obeyed – by now you know how to ensure that it is!

THE RECALL

This exercise will teach your dog to come to you immediately you call him, whenever and wherever you do so. The important word here is *immediately* – not when he feels like coming, not when there is nothing more interesting to do, but instantly and fast, no matter what he is doing or what distractions there are about. For your dog to become reliable at this, you need an enormous amount of self-discipline in the early stages. There will be many occasions when you will require your pup's presence, but unless you can be one hundred per cent certain that he will come to you, you must not call him. Remember that once your dog is allowed to ignore or disobey a command, he has learned a lesson – in this case that when you call him he may come or not as he chooses. If you are not in a position to enforce the recall command, do not give it. Rather go to your pup, or wait until he comes to you.

However, having said that, there will be many occasions when your pup is going to want to come to you, so there will be plenty of opportunities for you to teach this exercise. Make sure you always give the recall command in a friendly tone of voice, and never be tempted to threaten or bully the pup. You can be firm as well as being friendly – no self-respecting dog will want to come to someone who threatens or shouts at him. Every time your pup is on the way towards you, use his name and the command 'come'. Once he reaches you, make a big fuss of him. For this training to succeed, he must associate the act of coming to you with a very pleasant experience.

One of the first opportunities you will have to use the recall is when you feed him. He will very soon realise that he is about to be fed, recognising the sound of his meal being prepared, or the sight of his dish in your hand. Try to ensure that at the moment he realises that a meal is in the offing, he is some distance away from you, so that as he comes running towards you in anticipation of his food, you can use your recall command. Once he reaches you, take time to praise him for coming, before offering his food.

If your relationship develops as it should, you will find it more and more difficult to get away from your puppy. Given the opportunity, he will want to be with you as much as possible. When you get to this stage, you will need to enlist some help. Get someone whom the puppy knows to hold him by the collar whilst you move away with his food

Fig 37 Once released, Belle cannot wait to reach her tugger.

dish. Ask that person to release the puppy as soon as you call him. If he is squirming and doing his best to get away to you, so much the better. Don't tease him with his food – as soon as you have praised him for coming you must give him his meal and let him enjoy it in peace.

As long as you have always praised him well before allowing him to have his food, you should have no difficulty in repeating this exercise at times when food is not available. In this case you substitute his tugger as his reward. You can gradually move outside, and increase the distance between you and your helper, so that your pup has a longer distance to travel before reaching you. As long as you make it well worth his while to come to you, by making a fuss of him and playing games with him, you should have no difficulty with training the recall.

If at any time you notice a lessening of his enthusiasm to come to you, go back to calling him over very short distances, with tremendous praise when he reaches you. Don't make the mistake of grabbing him when he does arrive, but let him jump around and enjoy being with you. He must not associate coming to you with bcing confincd, so oncc hc has comc to you and had his game, set him free. There will inevitably be times when you have to confine him, but so long as the number of times he is released after coming for his game vastly outnumber the times he is confined after coming to you, his enthusiasm should not waver. Again, if you have carried out this training correctly and with enthusiasm you should find it extremely difficult to get away from him.

Later on, when he is lead-trained, you can use the lead to 'reel' him in when you call him. If you feel it necessary, you can then progress to a long line attached to his collar. With this, you can take him to places where there are interesting distractions. Allow him to wander at will, then when you call him, use the line to ensure that he comes to you smartly. Every time he comes he should be more or less throwing himself at you in anticipation of your praise and a game with his tugger. Don't begrudge the time you give to these games.

Eventually you will perhaps want to introduce an element of formality into the recall, and require your dog to sit in front of you when he is recalled. Wait until he is coming to you confidently and keenly before you start to formalise the exercise. He should already be familiar with the 'sit' command, so combining the two exercises should present no problems. Keep him in the sit for only a second to start with, then give him his game. Once you have started to introduce this formality, don't make every recall a formal one. Continue to include the fun recalls in his training schedule. As your dog matures and has learned to come when called, don't make the mistake of calling him only when you want to do something with him. Make sure you always include a few fun recalls during your daily exercise, to maintain his enthusiasm – call him to you just for the sheer pleasure of his company.

LEAD TRAINING

Sooner or later you will need to teach your dog to walk properly on the lead. By properly, I mean walking at your side, at the pace you dictate, not pulling you along nor dragging behind. By convention dogs are normally taught to walk on

Fig 38 The long line used to reel in Angus in the face of distractions.

Fig 39 Angus is rewarded with his tugger after the recall.

Fig 40 Angus sits in front after the recall, before being rewarded with his tugger.

the handler's left-hand side. The most comfortable and practical position is for the dog's shoulder to be close to and approximately level with his handler's left knee. This is known as the *heel* position, and the dog is said to be *walking to heel*.

Although this exercise can be started with puppies, it is better left for some weeks. A puppy does not require formal exercise on the lead – he should get sufficient exercise playing in the house and garden and with the other exercises which you will be teaching him. Care must be taken not to overdo the heel-work training, as it can become very boring, and tiring for a puppy. Be sure to keep your sessions very short.

Before you can start heel-work training, you must accustom your pup to the feel of a lead attached to his collar. Make sure it is a lightweight lead, suitable for his size. Like the collar he will be wearing, it will not be a heavy adult-sized lead. For the first few times that you attach the lead to his collar, choose an occasion when he has something else on his mind – mealtimes would be an ideal choice. Simply clip the lead to his collar without making a fuss, hold the end of the lead and feed him as normal. If he should be irritated by the additional weight of the lead, or annoyed at feeling confined, the enjoyment of his food should distract him. Once he is happily accepting his lead being attached, you can proceed to the next stage.

Gaining his Attention

To gain his full attention, get him to sit by your left side, and have his tugger in your hand. The use of his name plus the sight of his tugger should make him look up at you. If he attempts to jump up for his tugger, use your 'leave' command gently. Don't be harsh with him, or he will learn to associate this training with unhappiness. If you have to start again, take your time and settle him down so that he sits quietly by your side looking up at you. As soon as you reach this position, praise him and release him, then give him a good game with his tugger. If you have carried out the earlier tugger play correctly, he should by now realise that he may play with his tugger only when you say so.

Gradually you can increase the time you ask him to sit and give his attention to you up to about a minute. A suitable command for this part of the exercise might be 'look'. You should not attempt to move from this stationary position until your dog is ready to give you his full attention for at least a minute.

Walking Together

The lead must hang loosely between you. It is there to prevent too much movement on his part once you start walking. Since he already knows what 'sit' means, there should be no need to use the lead at present. Think of it in terms of a mooring rope, limiting the dog's range of movement if he should decide to escape. When you feel he is ready to progress organise yourself with the lead in one hand and the tugger in the other. Hold the lead by passing the loop over your thumb. Don't on any account wrap the lead round your hand – if your dog should decide to lunge ahead you may suffer considerable damage to your hand. If the lead is too long to manage comfortably, get a shorter one, but remember it must be long enough to hang loosely between you.

Make sure that your dog can see his

Fig 41 Angus sits at heel, the tugger maintaining his attention.

Fig 42 The thumb should pass through the loop in the lead.

tugger, but don't tease him with it. As you step off on your left foot, give the command 'heel', and walk steadily forward for perhaps half a dozen steps, praising your dog as he moves with you. Release him and give him a game with his tugger. The sight of his tugger moving off should ensure that your dog keeps up with it. If in his enthusiasm he surges ahead, stop, put him back in the sit position at your side and start again, after getting his attention. He will soon learn that the only way to earn his tugger is to stay by your side.

If, as occasionally happens, he fails to move forward with you (because you have so impressed the importance of 'sit' on him), carry on walking and give a little jerk on the lead. As soon as he starts to move, give plenty of praise so that he realises that at this point it is permissible to move from the sit position. Make sure that it is a jerk, immediately released, and not a pull, because that could encourage him simply to pull against you. If necessary you can tease him a little with his tugger if he seems unsure whether to move or not. Once he has moved forward a few steps with you, praise him, then release him and have a game.

At this stage it may seem an unnatural position for your dog to be in, with his head turned to look at you. Remember that he is learning, and must give his full attention to you whilst he is learning how to walk in the correct position. Later on when he has learned all this, and you have dispensed with his tugger (but not for a long time yet), he will be able to keep to the correct position and

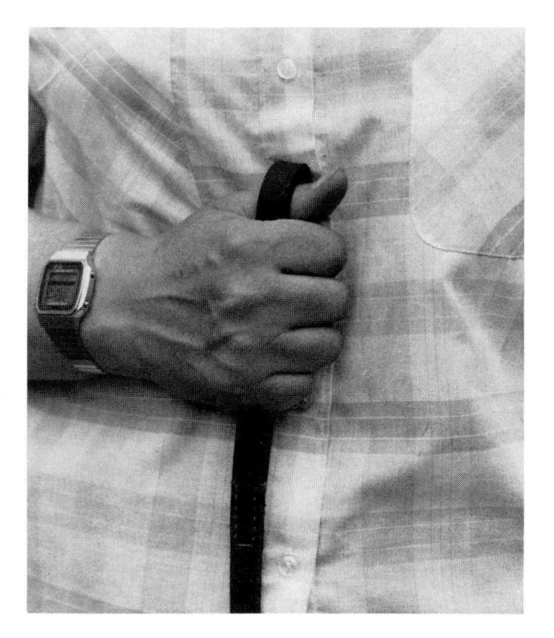

Fig 43 The correct way to hold the lead.

Fig 44 Angus learning to walk to heel, the tugger maintaining his attention on his handler.

Fig 45 Lulah shows the correct heel position, now looking ahead and walking on a loose lead.

give sufficient attention to you whilst being aware of his general surroundings. For the time being, however, concentrate on keeping his full attention on you.

You can repeat this exercise two or three times, on several occasions through the day. If you can keep your dog's attention for half a dozen paces, then the next day you can try a dozen paces. Gradually build up the distance until you can walk perhaps fifty yards with your dog maintaining position and concentration. You will not reach this stage overnight, so be patient and proceed slowly, taking care not to bore your dog. If your early training with the tugger was done well, your dog should want his tugger badly enough to keep his eyes on it and to follow wherever it goes. Make sure that it continues to be a sufficient incentive, by making the game you give him each time he walks correctly to heel well worth his while. This exercise has to be trained with a little work and a lot of play.

Circles and Turns

Once your dog can walk in a straight line with you, you can start to introduce large circles, first to your right, then later to your left. Make the circles very large to start with, so that your dog will hardly notice the difference from a straight line. In this way he will be able to maintain his position with little extra effort. As you gradually make the circles smaller, he will have to make more and more effort to keep in position. Make sure you continue to keep his attention on you, via his tugger, and reward him well for each success.

The next step is to introduce turns. Start off by walking straight ahead, then turn to your right. This will seem like a right circle, which your dog already knows, but instead of continuing to circle, walk on in a straight line, at right angles to the direction in which you started. When your dog has learned this lesson, you can repeat the procedure turning to your left. Later still you can introduce an about turn, by continuing to turn to your right until you are walking back in the direction whence you came.

All this will take several weeks to instil into your dog. Don't try to rush him, but make sure each stage is thoroughly mastered before going on to the next. It is very easy to bore a dog with heel-work, so keep each session very short, and be very generous with both your praise and your rewards. The turns that you teach your dog may seem exaggerated for normal walking, but the idea is to keep your dog attentive, so that it becomes automatic for him to maintain the heel position no matter where or how you walk.

The Sit at Heel

Once he is walking well to heel, you can teach him to sit when you stop walking. He already knows the command 'sit', so when you halt, give the command and be prepared to help him into the sit for the first few times. To do this you will have to transfer both the lead and the tugger to your right hand, leaving your left hand free to push his backside into the sit, at the same time raising your right hand (with his tugger) above his head. As he looks up, apply slight pressure to his backside and he should obey the 'sit'

Fig 47 . . . nearly there . . .

Fig 46 At the halt, Lulah is helped into the sit . . .

Fig 48 . . . the sit completed.

command without any problems. With careful practice, it should eventually become automatic for your dog to sit by your left side when you halt. This is a stable, comfortable position, where your dog can be alert to his surroundings, and leave you free to do whatever you need to do, whether it be checking the security of a door, talking to a friend, or indeed talking to a potential miscreant. As your dog becomes more and more competent at walking to heel, you can gradually make his tugger less visible, until it is concealed within your hand. Eventually, you will be able to keep it in your pocket, but don't rush to dispense with it. Always have it with you when you train, so that your dog knows he will always get his reward.

If you feel it necessary to teach your dog to walk to heel off the lead, don't even consider it until he is thoroughly competent at walking on the lead. Go back to the beginning and start with just a few paces forwards using the tugger to attract his attention. Slowly build up the distance, and introduce turns as you did in teaching heel-work on the lead.

Once you reach the stage where your dog is walking well to heel so that you are using heel-work in a work situation, don't neglect the heel-work training. If you use heel-work only when you are going somewhere, so that the fun and reward is lacking, your dog may soon become disinterested and careless. Continue to include some training in your schedule, so that at least some heel-work remains fun and is well rewarded.

SOCIALISATION

Whilst you are training all these control exercises, you will have ample opportunity to take your puppy out and about. It is important to get him used to meeting people and other dogs, and to make sure he becomes accustomed to various sights and sounds, so that later when he is in serious training he can concentrate on the job in hand and not worry about strange happenings. This process of socialisation is vitally important and must be undertaken carefully and sensibly. For instance, your pup must be introduced to traffic noises, but don't make his first introduction a trip along a busy main road. Rather take him into a quiet side street, where there will be only a few vehicles passing in the distance. You can then gradually progress to busier streets until eventually he will be quite happy to walk with you along the main road, should it be necessary.

Similarly, introduce him gradually to people, beginning with a few reliable friends, and eventually working up to a trip to the local market. He will be able to cope with crowds if he is given the opportunity to get used to them slowly. As his experience widens you can include visits to the railway and bus stations, a local building site, or collecting the children from school. Use whatever opportunities there are in your locality to introduce as wide a variety of experiences as possible.

At the same time, be careful not to overwhelm your puppy – make sure he is never allowed to become afraid of a situation. If you take every new experience slowly, there should be no problems. Never make an issue if he seems unsure, but give him time to adjust. If you are calm and matter-of-fact, he will take his cue from you and will trust you not to allow anything frightening to happen to him. If a situation should develop where it is obvious that your puppy might reasonably be expected to be afraid, get him out quickly, distracting him as much as possible from the experience. Later on, when you re-introduce that particular situation, do so very carefully. If you ensure that your puppy meets as wide a variety of situations as possible and never has a frightening experience, he should be able to cope with whatever experiences he meets once he starts to work for you. In this way his ability should not be marred by worry about strange situations.

USES OF CONTROL EXERCISES

The exercises taught so far are to enable you to control your dog absolutely, before proceeding to the man-work exercises, should you wish to do so. However even at this level of training, your dog can undertake certain protection duties. Since your dog will now walk properly to heel, he can safely accompany you if, for instance, you have to carry large sums of money to and from the bank. The presence of a large dog should deter all but the most determined of attackers.

The fact that he is fully under control means that you don't have to worry about him, but can give your attention to your surroundings so that, should you spot anything suspicious, you can take evasive action if necessary. Since your bank is likely to be in a busy main street, you certainly could not take an uncontrollable dog with you. By the time you had tried to stop him knocking someone over, disentangled yourself from the next lamp-post, recovered from being dragged almost under the wheels of a bus, the chances are that you would have dropped the money you were carrying – you certainly would not be allowed inside the bank for fear of frightening away all its other customers. With your trained dog, none of these hazards need arise. You can walk calmly and safely along any high street.

An obedient dog can accompany you when you answer the door-bell. If when you open the door, your dog dashes out to chase the cat from next-door for instance, he will not be much use to you. Equally he will be useless if he refuses to come to the door with you. It may well be a friend who is visiting, in which case your dog is not needed. On the other hand it may be someone less desirable. A door-to-door salesman is much less likely to try to put a foot in the door if

Fig 49 Lulah in the correct position when her handler opens the door to a stranger.

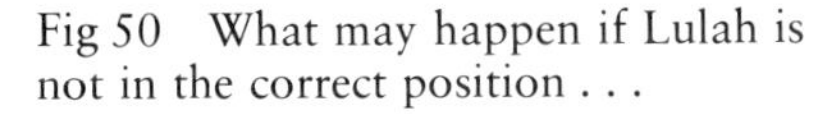

Fig 50 What may happen if Lulah is not in the correct position . . .

Fig 51 . . . the stranger is able to shut her out.

there is a dog sitting beside you, just about where he would wish to place his foot.

When you use your dog in this kind of situation, think about where you will place the dog. For maximum effect, he should be next to you, or slightly in front. He should not be allowed to go behind the caller. In this situation it would be easy for the caller to push his way into the house, and shut the door with the dog outside, thus leaving you completely unprotected.

Similarly, if you are walking in the park, you will most likely wish to allow you dog to run free and enjoy himself. If you have trained him correctly, and built up a good relationship with him, he is unlikely to wander very far away from you, and as long as he comes immediately when you call him, his presence by your side can at least give you moral support should you be approached by someone whose intentions are unclear. In most cases if you are approached, it will be by someone who wishes to ask for directions, or for the time, or for a light. However, in the less than perfect world in which we live, it is as well to be prepared for an approach by someone whose intentions are not so innocent. A well-trained dog by your side should not upset someone who wishes you no harm. By the same token, your dog's presence may well cause someone who does intend you harm to think again.

By now you should have sufficient control over your dog so that you can

Fig 52 Lulah left in the sit to look after the valuables at a picnic.

take him with you wherever dogs are allowed. He should behave beautifully in whatever situation you find yourselves, and should cause a nuisance to no reasonable person. If you can honestly say that you have reached this stage, then you have a companion of whom you can be rightly proud. If there are any defects in your dog's performance, you need to go back and repeat the training exercises until he reaches the standard of which he is undoubtedly capable.

5 The Speak on Command

Whilst many dogs will instinctively bark at a threatening situation, it can be very useful to teach a dog to bark, or *speak* on command. You can then ensure that your dog will speak whenever a situation occurs which you consider threatening. There may be occasions on which your dog might not consider a bark necessary, but where you might find his bark most useful. Apart from the obvious use as a deterrent or warning, you might perhaps be injured in an unfrequented place, and wish to attract help. You could of course shout, but the chances are that a dog's bark will last longer and carry further than your voice.

THE SPEAK

The age at which puppies first start to use their bark varies, from as early as a few weeks, to several months old. You will need to watch for these first barks, and to see what kind of stimulus sets him off. It may be that he will bark to get your attention (these are usually the early barkers), or when someone knocks at the door, or at the sound of strange footsteps after dark. Whatever sets him off, your response should be the same. Encourage him lavishly, using the command 'speak' (or whatever command you have chosen). It is most important not to chastise his early attempts at barking, however inconvenient the time or place may be to you (or to your neighbours!). Eventually you will be able to silence him when he has barked for long enough, or when barking is not appropriate, but for now you must tolerate his early attempts. If a dog is chastised for barking in the early stages of training, it may inhibit him to such an extent that it becomes difficult if not impossible to get him to bark on command.

Using a Trigger

Once you have discovered what triggers your pup to bark naturally, use every opportunity, and if necessary create opportunities, to reinforce your chosen command with lots of praise. If, for instance, it is a knock at the door that sets him off, then enlist the help of family and friends. Ask your chosen helper to knock at the door, so that when your pup barks at the sound, you can give your command and praise him. Then you can ask your helper to repeat the process. Children especially seem to enjoy this game, and often it is not necessary to use an outside door – it may well be sufficient for the child to leave the room where you and your pup are, and to knock at that door.

After the first few attempts, you will need to arrange things so that you can see your helper, though your dog should not be able to see him. You can then give your command just fractionally before your helper knocks on the door. This is to ensure that your pup gets the idea that he is to speak when you give the command and not simply because he hears a knock at the door. Because the knock immediately follows your command, this ensures that your command is obeyed.

Once this stage is successfully mastered, the next step is to ensure that your helper can hear you give the command to your pup. Ask him to delay knocking on the door. If your pup barks immediately, then your training has worked. If not, your helper must immediately knock, thus causing your pup to bark. In this case you will need to practise further the stage at which you give the command in anticipation of the knock. You will know that the knock is about to sound, but make sure that your pup does not.

Reluctant Barkers

If by the time he is nine or ten months old, your pup has shown no signs of barking naturally, you will have to find some way of inducing him to bark. If you can borrow another dog that does speak on command, this may well incite your dog to join in. Get your helper to make the second dog speak, and if your pup barks, give your command and lots of praise. If he merely looks as if he is thinking about joining in, try praising

Fig 53 Lulah is encouraged to speak by teasing with the tugger.

Fig 54 Angus has a game to encourage Lulah to speak.

him. This may well give him the confidence to bark. If this method does not work whilst you are with your pup, try tying him up. Make sure he cannot injure himself, and do not under any circumstances leave him with a slip-chain.

It may be that you will have to go out of sight before your pup will bark. If this is the case, return as soon as he shows the slightest sign of barking, then give your command and praise as before. Be careful how you return to him – you must return quickly, but make sure that the way in which you approach him is not in any way intimidating. You don't want to put him off just when you have succeeded in getting him to bark!

Another way to encourage a reluctant barker is to tie him up and tease him by making a fuss of another dog. Often the frustration of seeing another dog having a good time with you will result in your dog barking. If you use this method, you need someone with you to take charge of the second dog immediately there is any response from your dog, so that you can return to him and praise his efforts at barking.

Inconspicuous Commands

Once you have found the trigger to start your dog barking, use it as often as possible, so that you achieve a confident sustained speak. When this stage is reached, you should then gradually try to shift the emphasis from the trigger to your command as the signal for your dog to speak. Remember that during the time you are training the speak, your dog must not be chastised for barking. If at any time he should bark of his own accord, he must be praised. If it is an inconvenient time or place, you will just have to live with it for the time being.

When you have achieved a reliable speak on command (even if you have to stand on your head to achieve it!), you must make your command as inconspicuous to other people as possible. For maximum effect in a tight corner, you need a dog that appears to bark of its own accord. Only you and he should know that you have in fact given a command to speak. You could try gradually reducing the command to a whisper. Dogs have very acute hearing, so provided your relationship is right, and your dog attentive to you, he will be able to hear a whispered command whereas an approaching stranger will not.

Alternatively, you might find it useful to have a signal, such as clicking your fingers, or tapping your foot. If you decide to introduce such a signal, start by using it at the same time as you give your command, then gradually give it fractionally before you give the command, so that eventually the dog responds to the signal equally as well as to the command. You will need to practise the speak exercise in all sorts of different situations and locations, both inside and out, in daylight and in darkness. This is particularly important if your dog may be required to bark in places which have peculiar accoustics or echoes, for example in a very confined space or in a metal building. The first time a dog barks in such a place can be a somewhat nerve-racking experience for him, so don't try it until your dog is speaking very confidently on command.

The Cease

Not until you have achieved a reliable speak on command, with the minimum of encouragement from you, should you consider teaching your dog to cease to speak. The harder you have had to work to get a speak on command, the harder you should consider whether you do in fact need to teach the cease. If you decide to teach it, wait until your dog has barked long enough to wear off his initial enthusiasm, then give a very firm command 'cease' or simply 'no'. It may be necessary with a particularly vociferous dog to give a jerk on the check-chain at the same time. When your dog is silent, praise him, but in a more restrained fashion than normal, as you do not want to set him off barking just yet. If your dog was reluctant to bark originally, it is important to get him to bark again soon after you have silenced him, using the original trigger if necessary.

Once you have reached the stage where your dog will speak on an unobtrusive command, you can be confident that should a situation arise where a barking dog would act as a warning or deterrent, you will be able to use your dog in that capacity, whether it be to warn intruders that they have been detected, or to warn off a drunk who tries to become too familiar.

USING THE SPEAK

You can take the dog's ability to bark a stage further and teach him to search, or *quarter*, a given area or building, and to indicate to you the whereabouts of any person who may be concealed there. The idea is for him to use his superior scenting ability to locate anyone hidden, even in darkness, and to contain that person by remaining with him. He is to alert you to the exact whereabouts of the intruder by barking, so that you can home in on the sound even if you cannot see your dog. He may have found a child who is inadvertently trespassing, or a confused elderly person, or someone whose intentions are much more suspect. Once you hear your dog barking, you can follow up and deal with the situation as necessary.

To train this exercise, you need a person to act as the hidden person. It is important that you brief this person carefully, and that he understands exactly what is required of him, as it is he who will actually train your dog to speak when he locates a hidden person. Your dog must not expect, nor be given, any commands from you. His whole attention must be given to the hidden person (your helper), because if he were to look to you for help or praise, or even to come looking for you in a real situation, this could give an intruder the chance to escape, before you arrive on the scene.

Start by having your dog on a collar and lead (*not* on a check-chain, as you will be restraining him, not checking him). Give your tugger to your helper

Fig 55 Paul induces Lulah to speak by using the tugger.

and get him to make the dog speak. If he holds the tugger just out of reach and teases the dog with it, the dog should bark with frustration at not being able to reach his tugger. If necessary, your helper can give a command. You must remain totally passive – your only job is to stand still and hold the lead so that your dog cannot move forwards and grab his tugger. Don't worry if he jumps about, if you stand still he has a very limited range of movement anyway. Some dogs find it easier to bark if they have some freedom of movement, others quite happily settle in a position and bark freely that way. The important thing is that your dog barks vociferously at your helper. When he does so, your helper should come forwards and give the dog a game with his tugger. Make sure that it is your helper who moves, not the dog. Otherwise your dog may start to anticipate the game and later jump up at the hidden person, who may well be frightened unnecessarily if he is innocent.

Finding a Hidden Person

When your dog will bark confidently at your helper, the next stage is to get your helper to run a short distance and hide himself, teasing the dog with his tugger as he goes. The dog, still on his lead, should therefore be watching him eagerly. Your helper might hide behind a

Fig 56 Lulah watches Paul run to hide...

Fig 57 . . . a final wave of the tugger before Paul disappears from sight . . .

Fig 58 Lulah pulls her handler to where she last saw her tugger . . .

Fig 59 . . . when she reaches Paul, he uses the tugger to induce her to speak . . .

tree, or round the corner of a building. He should be in such a position that when the dog reaches him, he is clearly visible. Immediately give the command 'find him', and allow your dog to pull you after your helper. This is one of the few times your dog may pull you on his lead!

Don't try to check him but go at his pace if possible – obviously your own fitness is important here. Stop when the dog is about two yards from your helper, who should be facing the dog with the tugger in full view. If there is no immediate bark from your dog, your helper must induce him to bark as before. Again, your job is to anchor the dog at a suitable distance from your helper, who is playing the part of a possible criminal. As before, when the dog has barked sufficiently, your helper should come forwards and reward the dog with his tugger. After you have given the initial command to find, you should say nothing further. There must be no question of your dog looking at you – his full attention must be on the helper. Even if you only praised him, he would almost certainly look round at you. If looking at you for praise becomes a habit, he might well do it in a real situation, thus allowing a potential criminal to escape or take evasive action. You must train yourself to take an entirely passive part in the training of this exercise.

Repeat the sequence perhaps three

Fig 60 . . . and comes forward to reward her.

more times: let your dog watch your helper disappear, give the command and allow your dog to pull you in pursuit. Once he barks at your helper, he gets his reward. Don't be tempted to repeat the exercise more than about three times in any training session, however eager your dog may seem to be. It is very easy for this exercise to become stale, and for a dog to perform successfully in real life, he must be very enthusiastic. If you stop whilst he wants more, he will be all the more eager next time.

Changing Location

The next day, repeat the full sequence, but choose a different hiding place for your helper. Keep the session short and remember to keep silent except for your initial command. Continue in this way over the next few weeks. You will need to use your ingenuity to find different hiding places, according to the kind of area you have available. The only criterion at this stage is that although your helper is to conceal himself from the dog's view at the start of the exercise, once the dog has pursued him, your helper must then be visible to the dog.

Your aim over the next few weeks should be to introduce your dog to as many different potential hiding places as possible. Obviously, the kind of locations you will use will depend to some extent on the kind of territory the dog will eventually have to patrol, but do provide as much variety as you can. As well as trees and corners of buildings, your helper might hide behind bushes, bales of straw, oil-drums, a vehicle, farm machinery, a pile of packing cases, or a heap of sand or bricks. To start with he should be standing, then later he can sometimes be sitting, crouching, or even lying down.

He could also hide on top of a flat roof, a vehicle, a haystack, scaffolding, or farm machinery. If you can find a tree with a suitable low branch, your helper can climb on to it. He can also hide under machinery or a bush, or down a ditch. As well as using natural cover, you can make artificial *hides* if necessary. You will need a length of strong material, such as hessian or canvas, with a hem each end to take a broom handle. When the two broom handles are hammered into the ground, so that the fabric is stretched between them, the resulting screen will conceal your helper. Such a hide is easily portable, so you can take it to different locations to broaden your dog's experience. Whatever form of concealment you use, make sure that there is nothing that can harm your dog, particularly if you are working near machinery.

At this stage of training do not allow your helper to go inside a building, although by all means let him hide in a doorway, or in a corner formed by two adjacent walls. Empty buildings can have peculiar accoustics, and can also make your dog feel trapped, both of which will lead to a loss of confidence. At this stage that is the last thing you want to happen. Save any buildings to which you have access for a later stage of training.

For some of the hiding places you choose, for example a flat roof, the helper will not be completely hidden from your dog at the start of the exercise. This does not matter – he is hidden from the point of view of being inaccessible to the dog. Such locations reinforce the idea that it is the *presence* of a person which must cause your dog to bark.

As your dog gains in confidence in going forwards to find and speak at a hidden person, ask your helper to make the tugger gradually less visible, until eventually the dog will bark immediately he finds the person. He should then still be rewarded with a game. If there is the slightest hesitation on the dog's part, the tugger must be revealed and the dog once again induced to bark immediately.

Looking ahead to when you will be using this exercise in a real situation, if you think it will be appropriate to warn or challenge a possible hidden person, now is the time to start such a warning. Before you give your command to 'find him', you might shout something like, 'Come out and give yourself up, or else I shall send my dog to find you', then give your dog his usual command and proceed as before.

Working 'Blind'

All this time your dog will have watched your helper conceal himself at the start of the exercise. It is very easy to think that the dog, having repeated the exercise a few times, has got the idea, but it is a mistake to proceed too quickly to the next stage. The easier you make the exercise in the early stages, the more reliable your dog will eventually be. For this exercise to become a reliable part of your dog's repertoire as a working dog, he must be both confident and motivated, hence the insistence on prolonged successes in the early days.

Only when your dog is confident and

highly motivated (and this stage will take weeks, even months, rather than days) should you proceed to the next stage, which is to repeat the exercise 'blind'. For this, go back to a location with which your dog is familiar. Before bringing out your dog, get your helper to hide in a spot which he has used before. Make sure he will be able to see the dog at the beginning of the exercise – behind a bush would be a suitable place. Bring out your dog, issue your challenge if you use one, and command your dog to 'find him'. If your early training has been sufficiently thorough, your dog should set off immediately to look for your helper. Once found and barked at, he should come forwards and reward the dog as before. If your dog should set off in the wrong direction, don't try to check him. After all in a real situation you would not necessarily know where a person was hiding. As long as he sets off as though he intends to find your helper, go along with him as normal.

When he draws a blank at the first place he tries, encourage him to try again (unless he carries on of his own accord) by repeating the command 'find him'. It is permissible to repeat your command in this situation, since he tried to obey the first command. The fact that he chose the wrong direction should not be held against him. However, if this time he sets off in another wrong direction your helper should immediately draw attention to himself by a shout or a brief appearance. As soon as the dog notes his position, your helper can again conceal himself and the exercise can proceed as previously.

If at the start of the exercise your dog does not immediately make some attempt to find, your helper must also draw attention to himself as above. In this case you will need to spend more time with the first stage of the exercise, that is allowing the dog to watch your helper conceal himself.

However, assuming success at this level, you can now gradually work through all your locations in this manner. Make sure that your helper understands that he must take action immediately there is the slightest hint of uncertainty from your dog. It is better that he should help the dog unnecessarily than that the dog should be left in confusion. Whilst you are working through all your locations with your dog setting out 'blind', include an occasional exercise where he watches your helper run to hide. You can also vary the distance over which your dog has to pull you before reaching the hidden person. Keep the distance short for the less familiar spots, but increase it for known locations – the distance will of course depend on your fitness. If the exercise is being carried out correctly you will be pulled at full speed!

It is important that you continue to work with your dog on the lead, so that you can anchor him at a suitable distance from your helper. If you can use a variety of helpers, this will be much to your dog's advantage – he will learn to locate 'a person' rather than one particular individual. Be sure to brief each new helper thoroughly. Introduce a new helper by going right back to the beginning, making sure that he can induce your dog to speak, then letting the dog watch him conceal himself, before eventally proceeding to 'blind' searches.

Building Searches

When your dog is going out confidently on 'blind' searches, you can start to introduce building searches. First of all,

Fig 61 Angus has located Paul hidden in the bushes and speaks to indicate his success.

take your dog into a suitable building – warehouse, barn, outhouse – and do a speak on command. You may have to work quite hard at this, giving a great deal of encouragement and praise, if the accoustics are strange. Your dog may not recognise his own voice at first! Once you have achieved a speak on command, get your helper to induce your dog to speak. Then let your dog see the helper run off and conceal himself elsewhere in the building. Give your command, and allow your dog to pull you to the hiding spot. Again when he barks, your helper should come forward and reward the dog with his tugger.

When your dog is carrying out this exercise confidently, you can proceed to a 'blind' search. Have your helper hidden, then take your dog into the building and proceed as before. The next stage is for you to start outside the building, letting your dog watch your helper run into the building. When this stage is mastered satisfactorily, you can then do 'blind' searches from outside the building. All through your building training, watch the effect it is having on your dog. Some dogs cope happily with working inside buildings; others find it inhibiting, in which case you must proceed very carefully and slowly, interspersing building searches with lots of outdoor work.

Slipping the Lead

If you have proceeded slowly and thoroughly with this area of search training, the next stage should present no difficulties. Go back to the original set-up and allow your dog to watch your helper conceal himself. Proceed as before, but this time as your dog sets off to find, allow the lead to slip through your fingers, so that the dog is on his own, although you will be following up. If there is any difference in the way the dog completes the exercise, you will need to do more training on the lead.

If, as it should, the exercise proceeds satisfactorily, you can now start to unclip the lead as you send the dog to find. Always follow your dog, but gradually increase the time it takes you to reach him. Instead of running at full speed, you can jog along, then later walk up. The idea you wish to implant in your dog's mind is that you arrive in answer to his bark. Therefore it is of prime importance that your helper sustains your dog's interest until you arrive.

When your dog is confidently sustaining his bark until you reach him, in a variety of locations, you can introduce 'blind' searches off the lead. At first you will follow up very quickly, then gradually slow down in order to build up the dog's speak. Obviously in real life you would follow up as quickly as possible in order to deal with whatever situation

Fig 62 Oops! Angus looks back at his handler, and Paul is able to escape.

Fig 63 Although Paul hides up a tree, Angus locates him and speaks.

your dog had discovered, but in case you should ever be delayed in reaching your dog, you need to extend the length of time you expect your dog to bark in training, to cover that eventuality.

THE QUARTER

So far your dog should have learned the kinds of places where an intruder might be concealed, and to remain with that intruder when found and bark confidently at him until you arrive. Now you need to teach your dog to search systematically a given area (to *quarter*), and to indicate the presence of any person concealed there. If the dog is allowed to rush around willy-nilly, he might perhaps find such a person anyway, but it is far better to teach him to do the job correctly. If the dog searches the area immediately in front of you thoroughly and gives no indication, you can be reasonable certain there is no one there to jump you, so you can move into that area and send the dog on to quarter the next area, and so on.

To start training this part of the exercise, you need an area with two fairly obvious hiding places, one quite close to your starting point, and one a little further away. The wind should not be blowing from the second hide to the dog at the start of the exercise, as by now your dog will, whether you have noticed it or not, be using his nose as well as his eyes to locate a hidden person. Take up your position with your dog, and allow him to watch your helper conceal himself behind the nearer hide. Then quickly take your dog out of sight whilst your helper runs to the second hide. Return, set up your dog as normal and send him to find. He should move out to the first hide, expecting to find your helper there. When he draws a blank there, repeat your command to find and point to the second hide with your arm. If your early training has been thorough enough, the dog should already be looking for the second hide. If you have arranged it so that the wind is blowing from the second hide towards the first hide and is therefore carrying the helper's scent towards the dog, he should be in no doubt as to where to go next. Indeed he may well locate your helper without any advice from you!

Once he locates your helper and barks at him, he should be rewarded by your helper coming forwards with his tugger as before. You can then move straight towards your dog. If there should be more than a moment's hesitation before your dog orientates himself and moves towards the second hide, your helper must attract the dog's attention. You will then need to return to the previous stage of training and consolidate at that level before proceeding further.

If all goes well, carry on working with two hides similarly arranged in different locations. Sometimes start with the first hide to your left, sometimes to your right. Remember to make sure that the wind is not blowing from the second hide towards the dog at the start of the exercise. If the dog can receive the scent of your helper, and therefore knows where he is, he will be confused if you try to send him elsewhere at the start.

Using Several Hides

Once your dog can confidently tackle a quarter involving two hides in a variety of locations, you can introduce a third hide. Use a familiar location to start with and ask your helper to run from the first hide to the third while your dog is out of sight. Again make sure that your dog does not receive wind-blown scent from your helper until he has reached the second hide. As he draws a blank there, direct him towards the third hide with your arm signal. At this point you can start to walk forwards. When found and barked at, your helper again rewards the dog as before.

Using this method the dog learns to quarter an area by working in a zig-zag pattern in front of you. As he clears each area, you can walk forwards in safety, so that when your dog does locate someone, you will not be far behind him. Once three hides are being covered confidently, you can add a fourth, then a fifth and so on.

All this time your training has taken place on fairly open ground, so that your dog will be clearly visible to you. He will be out of sight only momentarily when checking behind a hide. In this way you can continue to monitor his behaviour, and take steps to remedy any faults before they are allowed to develop. Should your dog at any time lose his enthusiasm for this exercise, you must go back a stage or two in order to rekindle his interest.

In training, never send your dog to quarter an area unless there is someone for him to find. Although there may be occasions once he starts to work for you when you ask him to quarter an area which subsequently proves to be empty, these should be very rare, and must very quickly be followed by a session in which the dog successfully finds a hidden person. A dog has to experience only two or three unsuccessful quarters before he starts to lose his enthusiasm, and a dog going out with only half-hearted determination is not much use to you. In training, you must make it well worth his while to quarter a large area thoroughly, by making sure that he is always successful, and that his success is well rewarded by your helper.

Difficult Locations

Only when your dog is capable of a keen and reliable quarter of an open area should you proceed to use an overgrown or wooded area, in which your dog will be out of your sight for much of the time. In such an area, it is important that your helper hides in a vantage point – perhaps up a tree – so that he can report on your dog's attitude during the times when you cannot observe it. Again if your dog is allowed to develop bad habits, such as

Fig 64 Two 'criminals' about to break in, are thwarted when Angus discovers them and alerts his handler by barking.

following interesting game smells, or generally doing his own thing, he will not be reliable. If your early training has been thorough enough, your dog should have only one thought in his mind, and that is to find the hidden person as quickly as possible – motivation is the all-important factor. Unless your dog is reliable on a quarter, you will never be sure whether his failure to bark on a real job is simply because there is no-one in the area, or because your dog has absconded.

When your dog is capable of a confident search and location, you can introduce a second helper, to hide with the first. If your early training has been correct, the presence of a second person at the hide should not present a problem. Occasionally a dog will be somewhat nonplussed when faced with two hidden persons instead of one. In this case, one of the helpers should be detailed to induce the dog to bark by the use of his tugger. Later you can have three people hidden together, again, only one of them should be responsible for making the dog bark, and for rewarding him, the other two being merely passive presences.

By now, your dog should be able to perform a useful service for you, and to quarter a given area, indicating the presence of anyone concealed within that area. Don't be tempted to think that because he can now do the job for which you trained him, his training days are over. All through his working life, he needs constant training sessions, always successful and always well rewarded by a game with his tugger. In this way you will keep his enthusiasm, so that whenever you need to call upon his services, you can be sure he is sufficiently well motivated to go out and quarter to the best of his ability.

6 Training the Man-Work Exercises

It cannot be emphasised too strongly that before you train your dog to bite, you must complete the training of the control exercises detailed in Chapter 4. Unless you have total control over your dog at all times, you should not attempt to teach him to attack. This group of exercises is not to be undertaken lightly, nor without full commitment on your part. Once you have started to teach your dog to attack, he cannot be untaught, and you will have to live with the consequences. However, provided you start with the right material and proceed sensibly and thoroughly, you should always have a dog which is perfectly safe in normal circumstances, and which bites only on command – a command which you give only as a last resort. Remember that if you allow your dog to bite indiscriminately or frivolously, you will be risking his life, because a court could order his destruction if he bites without good cause.

PREPARATIONS

Helpers

Before you can train your dog, you need to train your helpers, since it is they who will actually train your dog, by taking the part of criminals. Unless you are fortunate enough to have the help of experienced 'criminals', you need to do some preliminary work. First of all choose your helpers carefully. They must be confident and not afraid of your dog. Dogs react to fear in two ways – either they also become fearful, or they become over-confident. In both cases they then become unreliable. Secondly, your helpers must be capable of carrying out your instructions, and prepared to do so. You don't want them trying out ideas of their own and thus upsetting your training schedule. Thirdly they must be fit. They will be doing quite a lot of running, and taking the full weight of your dog pulling against them. Lastly they must have a good sense of timing, because this is the art of ensuring that the padded sleeve, the target for the dog to bite, is in the right place at the right time, either just within the dog's reach, or just beyond.

Sleeves

Before your helpers are allowed to start on your dog make sure that they can cope with the padded sleeve. It is worn on the right arm, as this is the arm that dogs are taught by convention to bite, being the easiest way to disable a criminal without damaging him unnecessarily. If the sleeve has a cover for the hand, it will have a strap inside the cover. This should be gripped by the right hand to keep the sleeve in place. If there is no cover, then the lower edge of the sleeve is again gripped by the right hand. It is important that the helper keeps a secure grip on the sleeve, so that it does not slide off his arm at the wrong moment. Sleeves are also quite bulky, and it may take some practice before your helpers feel comfortable wearing one.

Train your helpers to keep the sleeve-arm well up. So often you see 'criminals' running with their right arm trailing – this is a most unnatural position and does the dog no good at all. After all, how often do you see someone running away from a dog sent to bite him, with his right arm trailing? If you were really trying to escape from such a dog, you would certainly be running as fast as you could and that would mean your arm would be well up to chest height to assist your speed. This is where it should be when training your dog, if not even higher. If a dog has to reach for the sleeve, he will learn to commit himself to the bite. If he is to bite, he must be fully committed to bite, and not to a half-hearted nibble.

Whilst your helpers are becoming accustomed to the sleeves, you should prepare the sleeves for your dog. If they are of new leather, they need to be softened by the application of a good quality leather oil. They also need to have a sacking cover over the target area, that part which will cover the forearm. Make sure that this cover is securely attached, as you don't want it to part company with the sleeve at a crucial moment. You also need to prepare your flag or bar, if you have not purchased one.

Command

When you have prepared your helpers and your equipment, there is one further task for you. You must decide on the word or phrase you will use to command your dog to bite. Your choice may have far-reaching consequences. If, for instance, you were taken to court as a result of your dog biting, and if the alleged victim was able to say that you told your dog to 'kill him' or even to 'get him', this might tell against you. It would be better to use a less descriptive phrase such as 'stop him'. If the person after whom you sent your dog had just committed a crime, or you might reasonably have expected that he was about to do so, it would be reasonable for you to attempt to stop him. It might be even better if you choose a phrase which has no meaning connected with biting. If you choose such a phrase, it will also act as a safeguard against an unauthorised person inciting your dog to bite.

Now that you have made the necessary preparations, you need to find a suitable place in which to start training your dog to bite. It must be a secluded spot where you can be sure there will be no interruptions from stray dogs or people. In the early stages your dog's attention must be solely on your 'criminal', and if other dogs or people come on to the scene it could distract your dog. To start with you need only a small area as all your training will be done on the lead.

USING THE FLAG

As the handler, you need to be able to stand with your back to something like a wall. This is partly to give you a base

Fig 65 Coney, at eight months, is teased with the flag.

from which to work, but also to prevent your dog ducking behind you. The training will include much teasing of the dog in order to build up his determination to bite, and if done correctly, the dog will try his best to get to the sleeve by avoiding the restriction of the lead. Some dogs learn very quickly that it is sometimes possible by moving backwards to slip their head through the collar. If moving backwards for this purpose becomes a habit it could appear as a weakness to a future criminal, and is therefore to be avoided. With a wall behind you, the only way for the dog to move is forwards.

Take up your position in front of the wall, with your dog on a collar (not a check-chain) and lead. Make sure that both are of very strong construction, as they will be under considerable strain. Your helper should be in front of you with the flag, in such a position that the flag is just out of reach of the dog. This takes careful judgement, remembering that if you stand still, the dog can move forwards for the length of your arm, plus the length of his lead plus the amount he can stretch his neck. For maximum effect, the flag should be only as far away as is necessary to keep it out of his reach, so that he feels he has a real chance of grabbing it.

Your helper should tease the dog with the flag for a few seconds, by waving it in front of him and whipping it out of reach

Fig 66 Coney reaches high for the flag.

Fig 67 Coney's handler applies pressure on the lead to encourage his determination to hold on to the flag . . .

as the dog comes forwards. Your helper can use vocal taunts also. As this is an extension of the games with his tugger, there should be no hesitation on your dog's part in coming forwards with eagerness. You must stand still, but you can encourage your dog to make every effort to grab the flag. The length of time the teasing lasts needs to be carefully judged. It must last long enough to build up the dog's determination, but not so long that he feels he is on a losing game and therefore loses interest. You will be the best judge of the timing, and when you feel your dog's forward lunges are sufficiently determined, give your command ('stop him', or whatever you have chosen), and allow the dog to pull you a step forwards so that he can grab the flag.

Once he has a good grip on the flag you should again stand still whilst your helper pulls steadily against your dog. It must be a steady pull, not a series of jerks. The idea is not to make the dog loosen his grip, but rather to encourage him to strengthen it. If you judged the teasing right, there is no way that your dog is now going to let go of the flag. You can help his determination by pulling gently back on his lead, so that effectively you and your dog are having a

Fig 68 . . . and his determination is rewarded when he finally wins the flag.

tug of war with your helper and the flag. Obviously the strength of the pulling must be suited to your dog's ability. After a few seconds of this game, your helper should gradually loosen his grip on the flag and allow the dog to win it. At this point you must praise him generously, and after allowing him to savour his triumph, gently take the flag from him.

After returning the flag to your helper you should repeat the whole sequence again. Remind your helper that he should keep the flag high, so that at the moment of impact, the dog is moving forwards and upwards, which gives the dog the best chance of securing a good grip. Obviously the flag must not be held so high that the dog cannot reach it within the confines of his lead. End the session after four or five such games – on no account prolong the session beyond this number. If the training is being carried out with the necessary enthusiasm on your dog's part, he will be putting considerable pressure on his jaw and neck muscles, and until these muscles are developed, you must take care that they are not over-strained.

Your dog will undoubtedly be disappointed when you end the session, but that will make him even more deter-

Fig 69 John has to use two hands on the flag against Coney.

mined the next time he is allowed to play this game. Remembering your introduction of the tugger, these games with the flag should be a special treat for him, not something he is obliged to do. Only you need to know that it is in fact training!

If at any time your dog grabs the flag when you are not expecting him to do so, do not chastise him. Every time he grabs it, he must be praised. There must be no uncertainty in his mind that it is always right to grab the flag (this applies equally when he has progressed on to a sleeve). If you or your helper misjudge the distance or timing, the dog must not be punished for your mistake. If he is not to bite the flag (or sleeve), make sure it is out of his reach. Remember this also when you are not actually training your dog. If the flag or sleeve has been left lying around, and your dog picks it up, praise him for doing so before gently taking it from him and putting it away.

This short training session needs to be repeated over the next few days, thus building up your dog's confidence and determination. Gradually you can increase both the backward pressure you put on the lead and the length of time your dog must work before winning the flag. By now your dog should be so determined to win the flag that your helper will have to take a two-handed grip in order to resist the dog's pull. At

Fig 70 Bren, on the lead, is teased with the bar.

this stage every game should end in a win for the dog. Your leave command should not be used.

When your dog is taking a firm, determined grip on the flag every time he is permitted to do so, you can graduate on to the bar. Repeat the same sequence using the bar in place of the flag. The only difference is that the bar presents a slightly firmer target for the dog to bite. Again your helper should find it necessary to hold each end of the bar in order to provide sufficient pull against you and your dog. Until this stage is reached, do not be tempted to progress further – patience at this stage will pay dividends in the long run. Remember that the dog must win every game.

INTRODUCING THE SLEEVE

Assuming success with the bar, the next stage is to introduce a soft loose sleeve, with its sacking cover. It must be loose, so that the dog bites the sleeve rather than the arm on which it is worn. An arm-filled sleeve at this stage is too much of a mouthful for the dog to tackle. Progress in the man-work exercises must be in very small steps for ultimate success.

Once again take up your position in front of the wall with your dog on his collar and lead. Your helper, wearing the soft sleeve, should stand in front of you,

Fig 71 Bren's determination wins him the bar.

again just out of reach of the dog. He should tease the dog by waving his sleeve-arm about, again keeping it high. As before, when you judge the time is right, give your command and allow the dog to reach the sleeve. Your helper should resist the dog briefly and then slip his arm from the sleeve so that the dog can win it. The similarity between the loose sleeve and the bar should mean that your dog takes his usual firm grip.

It is most important that this first bite on a sleeve is successful, as it represents an important barrier for your dog – he will now have 'bitten' a person, instead of merely an article being held by your helper. Contrary to popular opinion, most dogs do not willingly bite people, hence the insistence on adequate prep-

Fig 72 Coney, on the lead, is teased with the soft sleeve.

Fig 73 Coney, on the lead, bites the soft sleeve.

aration. If for any reason this first bite is not successful, do not repeat it. Instead, you must return to the stage of using the flag, then the bar, for several more training sessions before attempting to use the sleeve again.

However, your early training should ensure a successful bite, and so you can continue the session with four or five more such bites, with your dog working slightly harder each time in order to win the sleeve. Keep the session short, and repeat these sessions over the next few days. Gradually build up the pressure you put on the lead, as you did with the flag, and always let the dog win the sleeve eventually. Your helper should keep the sleeve high, as before.

DEVELOPING THE CHASE

When your dog is biting competently whilst your helper is standing in front of him, you can start to make your dog work a little harder for his bite. Get your helper to jog slowly from your left to right in front of you, so that the sleeve-arm is towards the dog. He should keep the sleeve just out of reach of the dog, and make two or three such dummy runs. The next time he passes, allow your dog to pull forwards just before your helper reaches the point straight ahead of you. In this way the dog should take the bite in approximately the same position

Fig 74 Coney, on the lead, bites the sleeve as John jogs past.

as when the helper was standing still.

Although there is minimal difference as far as the dog is concerned, this is the start of his timing of the bite. He will eventually have to attack a moving target, and so must learn to get himself in the right place at the right time. By making the transition from a stationary to a moving target as easy as possible, you make sure that your dog will continue to succeed. Your helper should be careful at first to keep the sleeve still, in relation to his body, so that there is not too much movement for the dog to adjust to.

Biting from Behind

Continue to give your dog practice with your helper moving across the dog. As your dog gains in proficiency, you can gradually let him move forwards later, so that your helper has passed you before the dog gets his bite. This begins to simulate a fleeing criminal, so that eventually your dog will be able to time his bite correctly as he closes on the criminal. Obviously, the further you allow the helper to pass you before allowing the dog to move forwards, the further you will have to move to maintain contact. Once you have started to move forwards, do not check your dog, but let him pull you at his own pace. It will be only a short distance so you should be able to keep up.

Continue to apply backward pressure on the lead once your dog has a firm grip of the sleeve. He can be expected to work ever harder before winning the sleeve, although don't take this to extremes. You must ensure that the dog never loosens his grip on the sleeve until it is in his possession. At this point he may decide to drop it – once it is 'dead' it may be of no further interest to him. So long as he has already won it, this does not matter. The important thing is that he should never let go at this stage whilst the sleeve is still on the helper's arm.

Once your dog is competently tackling these cross-bites, the next stage is for your helper to turn away from you. He should again jog across from your left, but as he gets in front of you, he should turn and jog away from you. You should let your dog move forwards just as he turns so that the dog takes the bite from behind, as he would on a fleeing criminal. Gradually you can delay the forwards movement, until you have to take seven or eight steps forwards in order for your dog to reach the helper.

By this time, your dog should be developing a really determined bite. If at any time you reach the point where he is

Fig 75 Coney, on the lead, bites the sleeve as John turns away.

hurting your helper, you can be very pleased, but you must of course protect your helper by providing a slightly more robust sleeve. Move on to another sleeve only when necessary, and then only to provide just sufficient protection for your helper's arm. There is no virtue in facing the dog with a harder sleeve than is necessary. By making the bite as easy as possible in these early stages you will build up the dog's confidence and determination much more surely than if you test him to his limits.

At the same time you should be using several different helpers if possible. No two people move in exactly the same way, nor present the sleeve in an identical manner. Variety will give your dog useful experience. However, all your helpers must be briefed in the same way, so that there is not too much variation in the way they approach the exercises. If your helpers can watch each other, their consistency should improve. When you introduce a new helper, go back several stages so that your dog is on very familiar ground as he tackles this new helper. In this way your dog should experience no confusion or loss of confidence.

Training a Second Dog

If you are training more than one dog at the same time, it can often be helpful if the other dogs are tied up so that they can watch the one being trained. They can actually learn from watching, and they certainly get themselves wound up, so that when it is their turn they tackle the exercise with increased determination. If you do this, make sure that the dogs are tied very securely. Don't use a leather or rope lead, as it is amazing how quickly a dog can chew through one when he wants to join in the action. For safety use a strong chain fixed to a secure anchoring point. Also make sure that the collar (not a check-chain) is sufficiently close-fitting so that the tied-up dog cannot pull out of it and so escape that way. If a dog were to get loose during man-work training, it could prove a nasty experience for your helper if he suddenly found himself with two dogs biting him. Alternatively, the two dogs, both being wound up, might attack each other. Neither situation must be allowed to happen.

Slipping the Lead

Once your dog is confidently pulling you seven or eight paces forwards in order to bite the sleeve, the time has come to allow him to bite off the lead. Take up your position in front of the wall again, and hold him securely by the collar. Get your helper to stand in front of you and tease the dog. As you feel him straining with real determination, give your command and release him. He should not be aware that you are not holding his lead and should bite as normal. If there is any difference you must immediately return to working on the lead. When he wins the sleeve, you will have to rely on your control training to recall him to you. Remember that he must not be chastised whilst he has the sleeve in his mouth, so if your recall command is not obeyed, don't shout at the dog. Rather chastise yourself, because you should not be attempting to train man-work exercises with inadequate control.

After several sessions where your dog bites a standing criminal, you can progress to the side-bite, where your helper jogs past you, as he did when the dog was on the lead. This time, however, he can jog past at gradually increasing

Fig 76 Bren, off the lead, bites a running criminal.

Fig 77 Bren chases Paul as he runs across.

distances, thus increasing the distance the dog has to travel. Always hold on to your dog's collar until the moment you release him. Sending him *off his collar* in this way means that you keep control over the bite, without diminishing his enthusiasm. Finally your helper can start to turn away from you and you can gradually increase the distance he jogs before releasing your dog. At this stage he should still be jogging – later he can gradually speed up to a run. Don't, however, increase the speed and the distance at the same time. Change only one of the variables at a time.

Once you have built up the distance to perhaps a hundred yards, don't continue with chases over a long distance. By all means include an occasional longer chase, but don't waste your dog's and your helper's energy in running long distances. After all, you know your dog will chase, and you know that he can outrun a fleeing man. What matters is what he does at the end of the chase, so concentrate on keeping the bite confident and determined. Most of your biting exercises should be over relatively short distances, say twenty to thirty yards.

At this distance, it is important for your helper to attract your dog's attention before you release him – he can do this by shouting. It would be appropriate now for you to start to shout back. If you ever have to send your dog on a chase for real, the chances are that you will first of all shout some kind of warning or invitation to the fleeing criminal to give himself up. If you start this now, it will later serve as an additional reminder to your dog about what he is to do.

Fig 78 Keeping the sleeve high encourages a determinated bite, as shown by Rambo, the Rottweiler . . .

Avoiding Kicks

So far your 'criminal' has been co-operative and has done nothing to try to hurt your dog. A real criminal might well try to avoid the worst of the dog's bite by kicking him. You need to teach the dog how to protect himself from kicks, without loosening his grip on the criminal. To do this, your helper should aim to push the dog in a clockwise direction by using the flat of his boot against the dog's side. Once the dog has a firm hold, the helper should stop running, get his balance and then gently push the dog with his left foot. He should not aim to hurt the dog at all, simply to encourage him to move away from the boot. In this way he will learn to swing the sleeve-arm behind the helper's back, and therefore cause him to circle in a clockwise direction. Eventually the dog should automatically take the sleeve, and therefore

Fig 79 . . . and Angus, the Collie.

Fig 80 Angus swings the sleeve behind John's back . . .

Fig 81 . . . keeping himself out of range of John's boot.

Fig 82 Similarly, because Rambo has swung the sleeve . . .

Fig 83 . . . Paul will find it difficult to deliver a kick.

himself, behind the criminal's back. As the dog develops this art, it becomes more and more difficult for a criminal to keep his balance. Certainly with the dog behind his back, he will not be able to do much in the way of kicking him, even less to aim blows with a weapon.

Strengthening the Bite

By now your dog should be developing a firm hard bite, and no doubt your helpers will have asked for at least one change of sleeve! All this training will have strengthened the muscles in your dog's jaw and neck, so that he can sustain a bite for as long as it takes for you to run the hundred or so yards that he has covered to reach the sleeve. If, however, your helper's time is somewhat limited, you can strengthen your dog's bite in the absence of help. Tie the sleeve to a length of rope, and place the rope over a beam or suitable branch. You can take the strain at the end of the rope, whilst your dog is sent to attack the sleeve. By gradually raising the height of the sleeve from the ground, you can make your dog reach further for it. You can also gradually increase the thickness of the sleeve by padding it, first with a sack, then with a thin branch and later with a thicker branch to simulate a man's arm. This can be a useful aid to developing the dog's bite, but it should not be used to the exclusion of training on people.

So far, your dog has always won the sleeve at the end of each bite. He will not be able to do this in real life – your criminal's arm will not simply drop off! Now is the time to teach your dog to relinquish the sleeve whilst it remains on the arm of your helper. To teach this part of the exercise, put your dog back on the lead, and let him bite the sleeve. Once he has a firm hold, tell your helper to cease to struggle, and give a very firm 'leave' command. Your dog already knows this command from his control training, so that the command coupled with the lack of resistance from your helper should at the very least cause the dog to slacken his grip sufficiently for your helper to remove the sleeve from his reach. Since you have the dog on the lead you can prevent him from re-gripping the sleeve. Praise him, and reassure him that he has done the right thing. Now that you have introduced the leave, don't always finish the bite this way. More often than not your dog should be allowed to win the sleeve. Only use the leave sufficiently often to maintain control.

Fig 84 Angus strengthens his bite in the absence of a criminal.

Concealed Sleeves

Up until now your dog has always attacked a clearly visible target, the sleeve. Now it is time to introduce a concealed sleeve, so that your helper appears to have no protection, again simulating a real situation. Your helper needs to wear a close-fitting sleeve, with no hand cover, over which he wears an old jacket, so that to the dog there is no visible target. Go back to your position in front of the wall, with your dog again on his collar and lead. Your helper should slip the old soft sleeve over his jacket, and tease the dog before giving him a couple of bites to warm him up. Then he should tease him again, wearing only the concealed sleeve, and let him bite the concealed sleeve. Obviously you will have to use your leave command to end this bite.

When your dog will confidently bite the concealed sleeve from the front, he should be given the opportunity of a side-bite, then later an away-bite, following the same sequence as when first training the bite, at first on the lead, then off his collar. Of course this will take place over several sessions, interspersed with bites on the normal sleeve. Don't over-train on the concealed sleeve, as it is much harder for your dog to grip well, and too much of this training could weaken his bite. Having introduced the concealed sleeve, include it only occasionally in your future training. Most of your training should be on the normal

Fig 85 Rambo obeys the 'leave' command, whilst Paul keeps the sleeve very still.

Fig 86 Bren bites the concealed sleeve.

sleeve. This is not only easier for your helper to put on, and to relinquish to your dog, but it is also better for keeping your dog's bite firm and hard.

SEARCH AND ESCORT OF PRISONER

If you were faced with an actual situation now, you could reasonably expect your dog to chase and detain a running criminal, by holding on to his right arm, and to maintain that hold until you arrived, releasing his hold when commanded to do so. What would you then do with your prisoner? If he were co-operative you could ask him to accompany you to your base so that you could deal with him there. However, most criminals are not so co-operative, and even having been bitten would still try to escape or to harm you. You need to use your dog to keep the situation under control.

The Search

Firstly, it would be prudent to search your prisoner to discover if he is carrying anything which he might use as a weapon against you. This will mean you

Fig 87 Angus watches whilst the criminal is searched.

being in close proximity to your prisoner, and therefore vulnerable to any attack he might choose to make. You must train your dog to take up a position and to be alert to any such attack, so that he can come to your rescue if necessary.

After your dog has chased and bitten your helper, use your leave command to terminate the bite. Place your dog in the sit, and ask your helper to face him at a distance of two to three yards, and remain perfectly still. Command your dog to stay, whilst you carefully circle round behind your helper. Make sure that your dog does not move. When you return to him, praise him and release him, but keep him under control so that he does not attempt to bite the sleeve again. He now has to learn that he should not bite whilst the criminal stands still, which is why your helper must not move.

After a few repeats of this exercise, the next step is for you to ask your helper to assume 'the position', that is, to stand with his feet apart and his arms outstretched. This time as you circle behind him, pause briefly as if searching him, then return to your dog as before. You can then gradually extend the time until you do a thorough search of your helper, whilst keeping a careful eye on your dog to make sure that he does not move. Your dog should be watching your helper all this time. If at any time his attention should waver, your helper must attract the dog's attention by shouting and moving the sleeve as an invitation to the dog to bite. Once he has bitten, command your dog to leave and continue the exercise as before. If during your search of your helper the dog is given an occasional bite, he will watch the helper eagerly for the first signs of movement so that he has an excuse to bite. You must make sure that he only bites when there has been such movement. Also, be careful only to search from behind – if you were to step in front of your criminal, and thus put yourself between him and your dog, he would be able to grab you and use you as a shield against any attack your dog might make.

The Escort

Now that you can complete a detailed search of your prisoner, you must be able to escort him back to your base. After you have searched your helper, return to your dog. Ask your helper to put his arms slowly down to his sides and to make an about turn. Keep your dog under control by your side. Your helper should then start to walk forwards at a steady pace. You follow about three or four yards behind with your dog at heel. In order to maintain your dog's interest, the helper should turn after several paces and raise the sleeve so that your dog may bite him. If your dog expects a bite on the escort, he will again watch your helper eagerly for the signal to bite. In this way he will learn to concentrate on any prisoner you might have to escort, and should the prisoner attempt to escape your dog will be ready to restrain him. You should gradually build up the distance you and your dog escort your helper before the dog gets his bite.

As well as walking in a straight line, your helper should also make turns, following your directions. You and your dog should maintain your distance and position whatever route your helper takes. Make sure that your dog remains smartly at heel, and that his heel-work does not become sloppy.

In case you should ever have to escort two such prisoners, you should train

Fig 88 Angus in position to escort the prisoner . . .

Fig 89 . . . who turns . . .

Fig 90 . . . as Angus moves forward . . .

Fig 91 . . . to bite the sleeve.

occasionally with two helpers. They should stand side by side, about a yard or so apart. In this way they will both remain in the dog's line of vision. Carry out your search of one helper, followed by a search of the other. If it becomes necessary to sustain your dog's interest, one of them should offer him a bite, whilst the other stands still. Similarly, on the escort they should walk side by side, and again only one should turn and offer a bite, the other moving only far enough to keep out of the way. If you think it likely that you might have to deal with three prisoners, you can train in a similar manner with three helpers. Keep your helpers close together, so that your dog can easily keep them all under observation at the same time. You will have to warn any prisoners that you escort that they should not make any movements other than to walk at a steady pace, otherwise they will very likely be bitten!

Fig 92 Angus is left to watch Paul . . .

Fig 93 . . . who turns when Angus looks away . . .

Fig 94 . . . but Angus makes sure that Paul does not escape.

You may need to search an area where a prisoner, previous to being caught, might have hidden a weapon or evidence. To train for this eventuality, start as for the beginning of the search, with your dog sitting a couple of yards in front of your helper. This time you should walk off behind your dog, as if to search a possible hiding place. As soon as your helper notices your dog's attention is wavering, he should attract the dog by shouting and raising the sleeve to offer a bite. Sometimes he can offer the bite by stepping towards the dog, and sometimes by turning to run away. In this way, when your dog is left to guard a prisoner, he should maintain his attention on the prisoner in the expectation of a bite. Obviously you should not leave your dog on guard in such a manner for longer than necessary.

THE USE OF WEAPONS

Any criminal that you have to apprehend by using your dog may try to evade the dog's bite by using a weapon, or may try to beat off a biting dog in the same way. Your dog must therefore be trained to avoid injury from such weapons as far as possible, and to carry out his attack in spite of them. A stick is perhaps the most obvious weapon, but whilst a criminal would use the stoutest stick he could find, your helper must not use a stick which might injure your dog. Instead, start with a thin whippy stick or two strips of plastic taped together at each end. Both of these will make a considerable noise when shaken, but will not hurt your dog too much if they strike him. Your helper should hold the stick in his left hand, and give the dog a bite over a short distance as usual. When the dog has a firm hold of the sleeve, your helper should slowly raise the stick and wave it over the dog's head, making a noise but not hitting the dog. At this stage of training your dog should be so determined in his bite that he ignores the stick. He should also be swinging the sleeve behind the helper's back (if necessary your helper can remind him of this by using his boot), thus taking himself largely out of range of the stick.

Gradually your helper can bring the stick nearer to the dog, so that eventually he touches the dog with it. Later he can start to strike the dog gently with it across the ribs, only increasing the force he uses when it is clear that the dog has no fear of the stick. The kind of stick you are using will sting the dog momentarily, without damaging him. This sting is similar to a jockey using his whip in the final stages of a race – not to harm the animal but to spur him to further effort.

You could of course consider giving your dog a beating in the expectation that he will become so angry that he will attack anyone wielding a stick against him with increased vigour. If you could be sure of the result, this might be a reasonable idea. However, it is much more likely that once your dog has learned that a stick (or any other weapon) can hurt him, the thought of self-preservation will make him stay out of reach. Once he has learned to think of himself instead of biting automatically on command, you will never be able to rely on his reaction to your command – so make sure he never learns to fear the stick or any other weapon you use in training. You should of course make it a habit always to disarm your helper before either your dog is allowed to win the sleeve or you use the leave command.

Once your dog will happily accept the

Fig 95 John holds the stick in his left hand whilst Bear bites the sleeve.

Fig 96 When Bear has a good grip on the sleeve, John starts to raise the stick.

use of the stick whilst he is on the sleeve, the next step is for the stick to be used as a threat before the dog is sent to bite. The degree of threat must be built up gradually, and be gauged to your dog's reaction. If there is the slightest hesitancy on the dog's part to go for the bite, your helper must immediately drop the stick and make sure that the dog then takes a good bite. Next time, proceed more carefully. The stick should not be used against the dog, but merely to teach him to ignore such distractions. Remind your helper to ensure that your dog continues to swing the sleeve in a clockwise direction behind your helper's back.

After training against the stick you can continue with various other potential weapons. These might include a broom, a plastic sheet, a bucket (later filled with water), an umbrella, or a dustbin lid used as a shield. Remember that your aim is

Fig 97 Paul uses a dustbin lid against Gary . . .

Fig 98 . . . but Gary ignores it and goes straight for the sleeve.

not to hold the dog off, but rather to make him ever more determined to reach the sleeve. Your helper might also use an old jacket, first draping it over the dog's back as he is on the sleeve, and later throwing it over his head. You should be able to think of various other objects which might be used as potential weapons, and train your dog to ignore them. The important thing to remember is that your dog must not be allowed to develop a fear of such weapons, and hence a reluctance to go into the attack against them. So long as he has no fear he should not react in an aggressive manner when, for instance, a person using a walking stick raises that stick to point. He should react aggressively only when the stick is being used in a threatening manner.

Fig 99 Paul raises a jacket whilst Lulah bites the sleeve . . .

Fig 100 . . . as he brings it down Lulah continues to bite.

THE USE OF A GUN

Before you train your dog to attack a person wielding a gun, you must make sure that he is perfectly steady to the sound of gunfire (and sounds similar to it) in normal life. If you have socialised your puppy adequately, he will be accustomed to sudden and different noises. If you have been able to exercise him in country areas where the local farmer is a shooting man, or where bird-scarers sounding like guns are used, he will already be used to the sound of gunfire, and should take no more notice of it than of any other noise.

If, however, he has had no natural opportunity to hear the sound of gunfire, you must introduce it carefully. Start with something like a starting pistol or a child's cap-gun, remembering that all guns used in training must be adapted to take blank ammunition. Find a suitable open space and give the gun to your helper. He should stand about forty yards away from you. Have your dog on the lead and give him a game with his tugger. Whilst he is engrossed in the game, your helper should fire a shot. If there is no reaction to the sound, he should come about ten yards nearer and fire another shot, and if necessary repeat the process. Sooner or later your dog will indicate that he has become aware of the sound. He may decide that it is of too little importance to merit any further attention, in which case you have no problem.

If, however, he decides to investigate the sound, he should be permitted to stop the game long enough to check on the direction from which it came. It is your job to ensure that this is the limit of his investigation – since he is on the lead you should have no difficulty in persuading him to resume his game. Continue with this exercise over the next few days, with the gun being fired at varying distances, and with an increasing number of shots. The only reaction your dog should be permitted to make is a quick check on the direction of the sound. When he resumes the game with his tugger of his own accord, you can then proceed to repeat the training with various other guns, ensuring that he develops the same limited reaction to all of them. Your helper should not point the gun at you or the dog, nor use it in any way aggressively, but simply fire it into the air.

Occasionally a dog, who is not gun-shy with most guns, will exhibit an unfavourable reaction to one particular gun, usually one of low calibre. I remember one bitch who would go into a frenzy if a starting pistol was fired, but who was perfectly happy if a shot-gun was fired quite close to her. Dogs have particularly sensitive ears, and it seems that the pitch of certain sounds can hurt their ears to such an extent that the sound becomes unbearable. If your dog is otherwise steady to the sound of gunfire, but reacts badly to one particular gun, there is very little you can do, apart from avoiding that particular gun in training.

Once your dog is perfectly steady to the sound of gunfire, you can start to include a gun in your man-work training. Your helper should bait your dog as usual, firing one shot into the air and then turning to run away, at which point you release your dog to chase him. Later he can fire a second shot whilst the dog is closing on him. It is important that the gun is not fired at the dog, nor so close to him that there is any danger of his ears or eyes being damaged by the discharge. The gun may later be pointed at the dog, provided that he is far enough away not to be hurt by the shot. Later still your helper can come towards the dog, firing as he does so, and taking the same care. It is particularly important that your dog does not develop any fear of the gun. He must be prepared to attack a person with a gun without hesitation, so that a criminal has no chance to take aim and fire directly at your dog.

INTRODUCING VARIATIONS

By now your dog should have considerable experience of chasing and detaining your helpers in a variety of situations, although so far he will only have dealt with them one at a time. They may be armed with various weapons; there may be a clearly visible target for the dog to bite; or the sleeve may be concealed. Whilst you should be careful not to over-train your dog, he will need to continue a certain amount of training for the rest of his working life. Your aim should be to give him as much variety and experience of different situations as possible. For instance, you might place obstacles such as a fence or ditch between him and your helper, who might alternatively try to escape by getting into a car or jumping on a suitable platform.

Fig 101 The car provides no escape from Rambo.

Remember that whatever variable you introduce, the object is not to beat the dog, merely to give him experience. If, for instance, your dog has difficulty in deciding how to negotiate a fence, your helper should wait for him to succeed whilst you encourage your dog to find the best way over or through it. Once the fence is successfully negotiated your helper can proceed with the chase. In training, your dog must *always* win. In this way he is more likely to win when sent after a real criminal. If a dog becomes disillusioned by failure in training, he is not likely to put much enthusiasm into his real work.

In a practical situation, where you and your dog have to deal with one criminal, your two-to-one numerical advantage should ensure a satisfactory outcome, provided you work together as a team. However, if faced with two or more criminals, decisions may have to be made. It may be necessary, in the interests of safety, to allow one or more of the criminals to escape, at least temporarily. Whilst a certain amount of initiative on the part of your dog can add to your partnership, in the last resort he must accept direction from you. It would be dangerous if, for instance, he were to chase a running criminal whilst leaving you at the mercy of two others. You must remember that you have greater power working together than as two separate units.

Fig 102 Paul puts on protective trousers . . .

Fig 103 . . . but has to be helped into the jacket to complete the full protective suit.

Fig 104 Gary takes first the right sleeve. . . .

With this in mind, your training should include practice for both you and your dog in dealing with more than one criminal. As you train with two or more helpers, you can create situations which will show up any shortcomings in your ability to work as a team with your dog. You must take responsibility for any failure to deal adequately with a situation. Your dog must not be allowed to feel that he has failed – after all he can do only what you have trained him to do, and what you allow him to do.

THE FULL PROTECTIVE SUIT

It is possible to buy a padded suit which protects both arms and both legs of your helper. This may be useful in rare cases where you have decided that it does not much matter where your dog bites, but it can be of only limited use in training. It is cumbersome to wear, and your helper will have very limited movement when wearing such a suit. Your dog's training would therefore be severely restricted.

Fig 105 . . . then the left one.

CROWD CONTROL

There may be occasions when you are faced with several hostile people whom you wish to move on. In this case it would not be appropriate to send your dog to bite – whilst he was biting one person, the rest could either escape, or more probably attack you. If you can pursuade each of these persons that they are in imminent danger of being singled out by your dog, you can draw on their collective cowardice to each get behind another for self-protection. To achieve this, your dog must learn to threaten each in turn.

You need two helpers, both wearing sleeves, in order to train for this exercise.

Fig 106 Rambo bites the leg.

They should be standing about four yards from each other, and just out of reach of your dog, who should be on his collar and lead. One helper should bait your dog, then without giving him a bite, the other should take over the baiting. If you stand still, your dog should move in an arc at the extent of his lead, trying to reach each helper in turn. His frustration at not being able to reach either sleeve should make him take an extremely aggressive attitude, as he lunges at each in turn. Don't try his patience too far. After three or four such lunges, he should be given a bite on one of the helpers, sometimes the one on the left, sometimes the one on the right. In this way, if he never knows which one he will be allowed to bite, he will keep his eyes on both of them.

The next step requires careful timing. Using the same set-up, you should allow your dog to move a pace forwards. *At the same time* your helpers should move an equivalent pace away, thus maintaining the distance between themselves and the dog. Gradually your dog can be allowed to drive the helpers further and further back, before he gets his bite. Later, your helpers can stand further apart, so that your dog has to cover a bigger arc in order to keep them both

Fig 107 First John baits Bren . . .

Fig 108 . . . then Paul causes Bren to swing across.

under control. In this way he should eventually be able to drive a crowd back, by threatening each member in turn.

FOOD REFUSAL

There is one final exercise which you may decide to teach your dog, and that is to refuse to eat food offered by a stranger, or lying around away from home. It is possible that a criminal might come prepared to avoid being attacked by your dog by offering food which is either poisoned or doped. If the dog took either, his protection value would be negated. If such an event is likely to happen it would be worthwhile teaching food refusal to your dog in order possibly to save his life. However, you should give much careful thought to the likelihood of this happening, as the training is a particularly distressing experience. There is nothing in a dog's instinct which makes him see the necessity to refuse food when it is offered, and therefore to teach him to do so requires aversion therapy. This means pain must be inflicted.

If you decide to go ahead with this training, you must accept that it will affect the dog's whole life. He must never be allowed to accept titbits, and must be fed only by you and perhaps two or three other trusted people (there must be someone else able to feed him in case you

Fig 109 Lulah decides that the switch makes it unwise to accept the proffered food.

are ever unavailable). For obvious reasons the training must be done by someone other than yourself. Your dog should be on the lead, and your helper should offer a tempting morsel of food. As the dog reaches forwards to take the food, your helper must deliver a stinging blow to the dog's nose with his hand. It must be the *attempt* to take the food which is punished, not the eating of the food. You must say nothing, since your dog must learn to refuse food in your absence. Your job is simply to prevent your dog from attacking the helper should he decide to do so, and to praise him if and when he refuses temptation.

If a blow from the hand is not sufficient to make the dog very quickly decide not to take the proffered food, it will be necessary to use a thin whippy branch as a switch. This must not be seen by the dog as a threat (otherwise it could be confused with the training against a stick). Your helper should keep it behind his back, and administer a blow with it so swiftly that the dog does not see what has hit him. When your dog eventually realises that to take food proffered in this way results in pain, and therefore he refuses to do so, praise him generously. The training needs to be repeated with various kinds of food, so that the dog

Fig 110 Lulah about to learn of the dangers of investigating food thrown on the ground.

learns to refuse the offer of all food, not just a certain kind.

Later he must learn to refuse food left on the ground. Your helper should throw a piece of food on the ground in front of your dog. He must be in a position so that he can punish any attempt by the dog to reach for the food. Later he should be hidden behind a screen of some sort, with food on the ground just by it. As you approach with your dog on the lead, he must take action if there is again any attempt by the dog to investigate the food. This part of the exercise should be repeated with various kinds of food.

THE FUTURE

If you have been meticulous in your training and honest in your assessment of your dog's reactions, you should by now have a dog who is not only a safe companion but also a reliable protector of yourself, your family, and your property. Together you have undergone a fairly intensive training course which should have ensured that you work together as a team. Unless any particular problems arise (in which case you will need to return to first principles in your training), you will be able to relax more with your dog.

Fig 111 Lulah will now go to any lengths to show that she has learned her lesson.

However, that does not mean that your training days are over. Throughout his working life, your dog needs to be reminded regularly of just what you require of him. In particular you must continue to polish your control exercises. As your dog becomes more experienced and self-confident with the man-work exercises, you will have to work harder and harder to maintain your control over him at all times. Remember that when you took on the responsibility for your dog, you took on that responsibility for the duration of his life. Whilst a dog never seems to forget a lesson once learned, he can become very casual in outlook if not kept up to scratch. As well as ensuring that he never becomes a nuisance or a danger to anyone, you must also regularly review your dog's ability and attitude. If you discover shortcomings in either, you must be prepared to take appropriate action.

If you have enjoyed the experience of training your dog thus far, and would like to continue and indeed extend your team-work, you might like to consider entering competitions where your ability to work together will be tested. Under the auspices of the Kennel Club, Working Trials are run in various parts of the country. By teaching your dog various further groups of exercises, you will be able to reach a standard where you could compete at the lowest level. You need to qualify at each level before progressing to the next. Entering such competitions can become an enjoyable hobby, and will certainly serve as a spur to keep your training at the highest level of which you and your dog are capable.

You, as the dominant member of the partnership, have the task of deciding on how the future shall progress. Make that decision thoughtfully and responsibly. Remember that, unless you abdicate that responsibility, you have a choice, your dog does not.

Useful Addresses

The Kennel Club
1–5 Clarges Street
Piccadilly
London W1Y 8AB

The Associated Sheep, Police and Army Dog Society
5 Hare Street
Grimsby
South Humberside DN32 9LA

The British Association for German Shepherd Dogs
55a South Road
Erdington
Birmingham 23

The International Sheep Dog Society
Chesham House
47 Bromham Road
Bedford MK40 2AA

Index

Index

Also available from The Crowood Press

Working Sheep Dogs

Management and Training

John Templeton with Matt Mundell

ISBN 1 85223 003 7   235 × 165mm   128 pages
58 photographs and diagrams